THE MOST HAPPIEST
JOY ON EARTH

"The joy of the Lord is your strength."
— Nehemiah 8:10

THE MOST HAPPIEST JOY ON EARTH

A 30-Day Devotional to Discover Joy in the World Around You

BONNIE CRIBBS

ISBN 979-8-218-76188-2

ISBN 979-8-218-77557-5

Published by Joyful Story Press

www.JoyfulStoryPress.com

This book is not affiliated with or endorsed by The Walt Disney Company.

Printed in the United States of America by Amazon KDP

For every heart that longs to live in God's Joy —
may you find it in every season of life.

Contents

INTRODUCTION

Welcome, friend.

I've always believed that Joy is one of God's greatest gifts — not the fleeting, momentary kind, but the deep, steady Joy we can carry with us through every season of life. Over the years, I've learned that this Joy isn't reserved for mountaintop moments or perfect days and that true Joy doesn't even depend on "happiness." It's woven into the everyday — in a kind smile, a warm sunrise, a shared laugh, and even in the small details most people walk right past. It comes from knowing you are loved, that you are a child of God, and that nothing can separate you from Him.

Some of my deepest experiences of Joy have been born out of difficult seasons, when I was clinging to a desperate desire for hope. Others came in a magical place you might know well — Walt Disney World. As a former Cast Member (and a frequent guest to the parks), I spent countless days surrounded by the music, colors, and creativity of the parks. But the real magic wasn't just in the parades or fireworks. It was in the little moments — a child's eyes lighting up at their first castle sighting, a stranger offering to take a photo for a family, or the way Main Street smells like popcorn and confections.

Those moments reminded me of something Jesus said in John 15:11: *"I have told you this so that my joy may be in you and that your joy may be complete."*

I wrote *The Most Happiest Joy on Earth* because I want you to discover — or rediscover — that Joy for yourself. Not just in theme parks or vacation days, but in the world around you, right where you are. In these pages, I share stories from my time in the parks and the ways they've helped me catch glimpses of God along the way.

This devotional is designed as a 30-day journey. Each chapter is split into two days:

✦ **Day 1** — A story, scripture, and reflection to help you see God's Joy in a specific moment or experience.

✦ **Day 2** — A deeper dive into the theme, with encouragement and journaling prompts to help you apply it to your own life.

You can read one section each day, or linger as long as you'd like in a chapter that speaks to you. Don't rush. This isn't a checklist; it's an invitation.

By the time you reach the end, my hope is that you'll start spotting Joy everywhere — in conversations, in quiet moments, and in unexpected places. I pray you'll know, deep in your heart, that the joy of the Lord truly is your strength... and that it's closer than you think.

Walk with me, and let's discover the Joy waiting for you

BEFORE
THE MAGIC BEGINS

"Of course you're always happy, Bonnie—you live at Walt Disney World and practically go there every single day. If that were me, I'd be happy too!"

I've heard this sentiment more than a few times over the years. Every time, it makes me smile. I usually laugh a little and respond with something like, "Oh, trust me—I'm far from happy all the time. I definitely have my moments. But I am full of Joy—and to me, that's way bigger than simply being happy."

The idea that Joy only comes from a life where everything is perfect—that's foreign to me. While I've been blessed with a beautiful life, like anyone else, I've experienced heartbreak, loss, disappointment, and some really hard seasons.

But through it all, Joy has remained.

It's that kind of Joy—the kind that outlasts circumstances—that this book is about. Over the next few chapters, I want to encourage you, inspire you, and help you connect with the Joy that doesn't depend on your surroundings. The Joy that runs deeper. One that's rooted in something eternal.

You'll find stories here—some from my everyday life, most from the magic of Walt Disney World, and some from my most vulnerable places. You'll also find scripture, encouragement, and reflection prompts designed to help you think deeper, grow stronger, and see the Joy that's been there all along.

But before we dive into the pixie dust, I want to give you a little perspective.

There's an old saying: *"A smooth sea never made a skilled sailor."*

Let me tell you about some of my rough seas.

When I was 11 years old, my job as the big brother was to make sure my little brother, Kelvin (he was 9), didn't cross the road without me while we waited for the school bus. We lived out in the country and could usually see the bus coming down the highway a couple of minutes before it arrived.

On mornings when we had time, we'd sometimes run across the highway to play with our neighbor, who was right between our ages. That morning, I was sick and couldn't go to school. For the first time, Kelvin had to wait by himself.

He went over to the neighbor's house like we often did, and when he saw the school bus coming, he darted across the highway back to our front yard. A car going 55 miles an hour hit him, throwing him 155 feet. He was killed instantly.

I lost my little brother that day. My best friend. And I watched my parents carry a grief I can't even describe. Even writing this, I can still hear the loud moans of my mom as she grieved in agony. To this day, my dad says it was the hardest thing he's ever gone through.

And for years, I carried the guilt of not being there. Not protecting him. In my mind, it was my fault.

That was the first time I really knew what heartbreak was.

Years later, I experienced another kind of loss—this time, romantic.

Fast forward to a year after my college graduation.

Kathy and I had spent time together on my birthday—February 13th, the day before Valentine's. She asked me to stay and spend Valentine's Day with her, but I couldn't. My parents were already on the road, driving to Gatlinburg from North Carolina to celebrate with me.

This was before cell phones and last-minute texts. I couldn't just tell them to turn around or wait a day. I had to go.

As I was driving to meet my parents, Kathy was headed home to Mississippi. A truck crossed the center line and hit her head-on. She didn't survive.

We'd been engaged, broken up, and had recently started talking again. There was so much potential. So much healing in progress.

And suddenly, it was all gone.

Once again, I carried guilt. If I had just stayed like she asked... maybe things would be different.

I had lost the love of my life.

And then came 2010.

I won't go into full detail—but here's the short version:

+ I was diagnosed with diabetes.
+ A simple gallbladder surgery went sideways.
+ My house flooded a couple of days prior to the surgery.
+ A meaningful relationship came to an end.
+ And I lost my mom.
+ All in the same year.

It was a storm of grief, loss, change, and pain. I literally felt like I was drowning. I lost myself and regret the way I handled it all. And if I'm honest, it's probably the main reason I'm writing this book.

Because even then— *especially then*—I discovered how important true Joy really is.

So no, this book isn't about having a "perfect life." It's not about skipping down Main Street without a care in the world. It's about the kind of Joy that *lasts*. The kind that can shine even in the middle of grief. The kind that reminds you, when your heart is shattered, that "Joy comes in the morning."

I share all of this not to make you feel heavy—but to help you see where this kind of Joy comes from. It's not fake. It's not fluffy. It's not reserved for perfect lives or picture-perfect park days. It's real. It's resilient. And it's rooted in something far greater than circumstance.

If you're carrying something heavy right now, I want you to know—Joy is still possible. Hope is still near. And you're not alone.

Over the next 15 chapters, I want to take you with me on a journey—a journey through faith, encouragement, some everyday magic from the parks, and the eternal truths of Scripture. You'll find room to pause, to reflect, and to pray.

My deepest hope is that these pages meet you right where you are—and remind you that Joy is available no matter what you're facing.

As the song goes...
"There's a great big beautiful tomorrow, shining at the end of every day."

And I want to help you remember where that Hope truly comes from.

Let's dive into The Most Happiest Joy On Earth..

Chapter 1:

JOY BEGINS ON MAIN STREET

DAY *One*
MORE THAN HAPPINESS,
RIGHT FROM THE START

There's a moment on Main Street that gets me every single time. It happens just after I walk through the tunnel, right before I see the castle. I take a deep breath, the popcorn smell hits, and the music wraps around me like a blanket. No matter what kind of week I've had— all the feels come out.

There's no telling how many times I've walked into Magic Kingdom at this point. I'm sure it's easily in the thousands. For years I've been entering pretty much the same way each time. Intentionally.

Humming to the entrance music, I'll enter to the left side of the train station, walk through the tunnel and see how long it takes me to smell the popcorn. I walk by the flagpole, duck into the Confectionary to catch the sweet smells, then step back onto Main Street to peek around the trees and see Cinderella Castle rising above it all.

It's that moment of seeing the Castle that brings a feeling of happiness. It reminds me of the magnitude of what's present. It brings back memories. It's that moment that I can take a deep breath and the stress disappears.

This tradition that I have to take the same route each time prevents these moments from becoming routine. There's something about that first step onto Main Street U.S.A that I never want to lose. It's a moment of wonder, it's a moment of comfort - it's a reminder of happy moments that have happened in the past and brings excitement about what lies ahead.

No matter how tired, stressed or overwhelmed you might feel walking through those gates, there's a reminder of Joy that seems to find you the second you're in that moment. It's like Disney's way of saying "You're here. You can let go of everything else."

Sometimes I like to head to the square at the point where people turn the corner and see the castle for the first time. It's beautiful to witness folks seeing the castle for the first time that day. Smiles explode. Eyes fill with tears. Excitement is shouted.

Watching those reactions is one of my favorite things in the world. It reminds me that wonder is contagious—and Joy is meant to be shared.

Those moments are happy moments. But there's something even better than simple happiness. It's Joy.

Happiness is often a reaction to something good happening. Joy? It's a response to knowing something good is *already true.* Even if nothing around us feels it at the moment. Joy is much deeper than a cheerful temporary feeling.

God invites us into something much deeper than happiness. He invites us into Joy - not just when we're on vacation, but every single day. Psalm 118:24 reminds us *"This is the day the Lord has made; let us rejoice and be glad in it"*

Joy isn't about how perfect your circumstances are. It's about how grounded your heart is in the One who made the day. How you are loved. How you are made in His image. How He has a plan for you. How He sees you. How He provides for you. Joy comes from a deep recognition of grace.

Just like Main Street sets the tone for a magical day ahead, choosing Joy each morning can set the tone for the day. But in this case, it's not just a show set or a theme park—it's your life. It's your heart. And it's real.

Joy is a choice. Faith is a choice. And they're not always easy choices - but they're always life-changing choices. It starts with gratitude. With noticing the good. With believing that God has something good even in this very moment. It comes from recognizing the grace you've received.

Joy like this—this everyday, all-the-way-down-to-your-socks kind of Joy—might just be the Most Happiest Joy On Earth.

Joy isn't soft. It's strong. Scripture even tells us in Nehemiah 8:10 that *"The Joy of the Lord is your strength."* It's a power I continually want to tap into.

Just like you may have a list of all the things you want to do at Magic Kingdom, I encourage you to create a list of the blessings you see in your life. The good things, the aspects of your life that you are grateful for.

Looking for the good is a habit - a habit that must be fed. It also involves turning off the noise of the world (or the noise in your head) and turning up the background music of your heart. You know, kind of like Disney does as they set the mood as you walk down Main Street with the music you hear.

Let's start right now by helping you see the beauty that's around you. Grab a pen and your journal and answer these questions.

Take a breath. Let the background music of your heart rise. Now let's invite Joy in—right where you are.

As you journal today, may Joy find you just like it does on Main Street—unexpected, sweet, and impossible to ignore.

Pause + Ponder

1. What are three things that brought you Joy this week—big or small?

2. When you wake up in the morning, what's the first thing you usually feel? What would happen if you *chose* Joy first?

3. Where do you feel like God might be saying to you, "You're here. Let go of everything else"?

A BLESSING: FOR THE ONE CHOOSING JOY TODAY

May you wake today — and every morning after — with the quiet courage to choose Joy first.
May the background music of your heart rise above the noise around you.
May you feel the wonder of God's presence wrapping around you like a warm Main Street breeze.
And may your life overflow with a Joy so deep and contagious, others can't help but feel it too.
You're here. Let go. Breathe in His goodness, mercy & grace and walk forward with a heart full of Joy.

DAY TWO
LIVING IT OUT:
CHOOSING JOY FIRST

There's something about that first step onto Main Street U.S.A. that sets the tone.
It's not just the music or the smell of popcorn—it's the feeling that you've arrived. That something good is beginning. That the hard stuff you carried in is suddenly a little lighter.

That's what Joy does.
It lifts.
It reframes.
It roots you in something deeper than just momentary happiness.

Joy doesn't wait for things to be perfect—it shows up *in spite* of the imperfect.
It's a quiet strength.
It's a practiced posture.
And it begins the moment you decide to let it.

Psalm 118:24 says, *"This is the day the Lord has made; let us rejoice and be glad in it."*
Not because everything is easy.
Not because the day is flawless.
But because *God made it.*
Because *you woke up.*
Because *you're here.*

When we begin our days with gratitude—when we train our hearts to notice the good—we invite Joy in before the world has a chance to crowd it out.

It's like humming to the music on Main Street as you walk through the tunnel.
It doesn't change what's ahead—but it changes *how* you walk through it.

So what if we started every day like that?

What if Joy was your first response—not just your reward?

What if you walked into each day like it was a gift waiting to be un-wrapped—popcorn, castle view, and all?

Read

> *"This is the day the Lord has made;*
> *let us rejoice and be glad in it."*
> **— Psalm 118:24**

> *"The Joy of the Lord is your strength."*
> **— Nehemiah 8:10**

Reflect

Pause and reflect on the questions below—let them guide you into a posture of Joy:

✦ What typically sets the tone for your day? How might choosing Joy first shift that?

✦ Where have you been relying on circumstances to bring happiness, instead of choosing Joy rooted in God's presence?

✦ What would it look like to "walk down Main Street" with your heart today—to intentionally notice the wonder that's already around you?

Be honest. Let God meet you exactly where you are.

Respond

Try one of these small practices today to intentionally begin your day with Joy:

✦ Write a "Main Street List." Name 5 things that bring you delight—sights, smells, memories, people. Keep it somewhere you'll see it in the morning.

✦ Start your day with worship music. Choose a song that lifts your spirit and sets the tone—before emails, before news, before anything else.

✦ Say aloud, "This is the day the Lord has made. I will rejoice." Speak it even if you don't feel it yet. Sometimes your heart follows your declaration.

Songs for Today

✦ *"House of the Lord* — Phil Wickham

✦ *"Your Love Defends Me"* — Matt Maher

A PRAYER FOR TODAY

Father,

Thank You for this day—this ordinary, beautiful, brand-new day.

Help me to choose Joy before the world even has a chance to sway my heart.

Let my eyes see what You're doing.

Let my heart stay anchored in who You are.

Remind me that Joy isn't something I wait for—it's something I walk in.

And may the Joy I carry today overflow into everyone around me.

In You, Lord, this day is already good.

Amen.

Chapter 2:

CHILDLIKE FAITH IN FANTASYLAND

DAY ONE
FLYING ELEPHANTS AND THE KIND OF FAITH THAT SOARS

Fantasyland is where happiness wears mouse ears, dreams shimmer in sparkly dresses, and wonder greets you at every turn. It's where the unbelievable feels possible, where kids look up at royalty with wide eyes, and where even the most skeptical adults find themselves smiling without even realizing it.

My earliest childhood memory happened in Fantasyland. I was four years old, and though it's just a glimpse, I can still picture it clearly: me, riding Dumbo. I don't have a photo from that day—believe me, I've looked—but I can still see it in my mind. I'm flying through the skies, the castle rising behind me, and I'm soaring with Dumbo. I remember that feeling of magic, of possibility.

There's something undeniably special about Fantasyland. It's where wonder is worn like a crown. Kids fly over London with Peter Pan, pull swords from stones, eat in Belle's castle, and swim under the sea with Ariel. It's not just about rides or characters—it's about believing that anything is possible. Magic feels real here.

Two of my favorite adult memories in Fantasyland both involve Cinderella.

One was a little girl, maybe five, wearing a sparkling Cinderella dress. When she spotted the princess, she let out a scream:

"Cin-der-ella!!!" and sprinted toward her like she was reuniting with a lifelong friend. Her arms flung around Cinderella without hesitation. Her eyes glowed. Her whole face lit up. She wasn't just *meeting* a character—she was seeing *her* princess. It was real to her.

The second moment was quieter but just as moving. A young boy, maybe six, approached Cinderella with hesitancy. He was shy. He barely spoke. But Cinderella knelt down, smiled, and softly called him "prince." She told him he looked strong. And I watched his little shoulders rise as confidence and delight spread across his face. That moment changed him. I'd bet anything he still remembers it.

I've never forgotten either moment—because they reminded me of something we tend to lose with age. Fantasyland wasn't pretend for either of them. It was real...

Oh, to have that kind of heart again.

To believe without needing proof.

To trade our adult craving for control with wide-eyed, wholehearted trust.

In Matthew 18:3, Jesus tells us:

> *"Truly I tell you, unless you change and become like little children, you will never enter the kingdom of heaven."*

Children don't need all the answers. They don't demand explanations. They're curious. They're dependent. They trust. I've lost count of the times I've watched a child in the parks get startled or overwhelmed, only to instinctively reach up and grab their parent's hand. That's what childlike faith looks like—knowing someone stronger is near and grabbing hold without hesitation.

That's the kind of faith God calls us to have in Him.

But let's be honest—we tend to overcomplicate it. We try to intellectualize faith, explain away mystery, or wait for proof before we trust. Scripture doesn't say we need a master's degree in theology to draw near to God. It says we need to come like children.

Joy shows up in those childlike moments.
In the reaching.
In the wonder.
In the moments when we stop trying to control and just *cling* to Him.

Joy is in the way He calls us *His*.
It's in the way He whispers that our strength, our identity, and our future are held in Him.

But over time, we grow skeptical.
We let people and disappointments redefine us.
We lose that spark of trust.
We stop dreaming and settle for "just getting by."

But what if we didn't?

What if we returned to that childlike faith?
What if we believed—really believed—that God is who He says He is?
Provider. Healer. Comforter. Shepherd. Father.
What if we trusted again?

Childlike faith won't make life perfect. But it sure would lead to more wonder. Less stress. More hope. And much bigger dreams.

If you've felt disconnected from your faith—or like the wonder's worn off—maybe it's time to see with childlike eyes again.

Let's explore what childlike trust could look like in your life right now.

So before you move on, take a moment. Pause. Ask God to show you what your faith could look like through the eyes of a child again.

Pause + Ponder

✦ Where in your life do you need to trust like a child again?

✦ What have you stopped praying for because it felt too far gone?

✦ When was the last time you allowed yourself to feel awe or wonder?

✦ If you approached today like a child in Fantasyland, how would it look different?

A BLESSING FOR A RETURN OF CHILDLIKE WONDER.

May your faith today be light enough to fly, bold enough to believe, and Joy-filled enough to sing out loud—like you're riding a flying elephant.

DAY TWO
LIVING IT OUT:
WIDE-EYED FAITH

C hildren don't overthink trust.
They don't ask for credentials.
They just *believe.*

A child sees Cinderella and runs with open arms.
A child hears a promise and clings to it.
A child sees Dumbo rise into the air—and *believes* he can fly.

That's the kind of faith Jesus invites us into. Not naïve. Not mindless. But deeply *dependent.*

Adults tend to complicate faith with what-ifs and worst-case scenarios.
We want control. We want clarity.
But children want connection.
They instinctively know when someone is safe—and they *reach up.*

Matthew 18:3 isn't a poetic metaphor—it's an invitation to return.
To come back to a kind of faith that doesn't demand all the answers.
To let go of performance and embrace presence.
To trade control for *trust.*

Because here's the truth: childlike faith isn't shallow—it's sacred.
It knows where to run. It knows Who holds the map.
It finds Joy in the mystery and security in the arms of the Father.

And when we lean into that kind of trust?
Joy takes flight.
Our souls breathe again.
And faith becomes a little less about figuring it all out—and a lot more about *holding His hand*.

Read

> *"Truly I tell you, unless you change and become like little children,*
> *you will never enter the kingdom of heaven."*
> **— Matthew 18:3**

> *"Trust in the Lord with all your heart and lean not*
> *on your own understanding."*
> **— Proverbs 3:5**

Reflect

Let these questions guide your journal time:

✦ Where in your life are you relying on understanding more than trust?

✦ When did your faith last feel *wonder-full*—and what sparked it?

✦ What would it look like to take one small step of childlike faith this week?

_____

_____

✦ Write honestly. You don't need to have it all figured out—just start where you are.

_____

_____

Respond

Here are a few ways to put childlike trust into practice today:

✦ Pray like a child. Keep it simple. Talk to God without filters or fancy words. Ask. Thank. Wonder. Rest.

✦ Do something playful. Let your heart loosen up a little. Take a walk, color, skip, or sing loud in the car. Joy often sneaks in through the playful moments.

✦ Reach up. Visualize yourself reaching for God's hand as you walk through your day. Whisper, _"I trust You."_ Let that posture reframe your perspective.

Songs for Today

✦ _"Run to the Father"_ — Cody Carnes

✦ _"Who You Say I Am"_ — Hillsong Worship

A PRAYER FOR TODAY

Father,
I've let my faith grow complicated.
I've tried to control, to reason, to carry more than I was meant to.
But today, I want to come back—like a child.
Teach me to trust You without conditions.
To reach for Your hand first.
To believe again—with wide eyes and an open heart.
Let Joy rise in the simplicity of Your love.
And let my faith fly like I'm riding Dumbo again,
full of wonder and completely safe in Your arms.
Amen.

Chapter 3

FINDING JOY WHEN YOU FALL APART

DAY ONE
GRACE IN THE MIDDLE
OF THE MESS

It was 2:16 p.m., it felt like 102°, and we were somewhere between the Carousel of Progress... and a full-blown four-year-old freak-out.

The little boy in the stroller had the deluxe setup—snack tray full of food, a Buzz Lightyear balloon flying proudly off the side, and evidence of a recently demolished Mickey Ice Cream Bar smeared across his face.

He was living the dream... until that dream melted faster than his Mickey bar.

It was like someone said the wrong magic word, and bam—he flipped into full meltdown mode. Screaming. Sobbing. Chocolate cheeks turned to streaky rivers of sticky despair.

It's a scene that plays out daily across the parks. I've witnessed it more times than I can count. Sometimes a parent will look at me, flustered, apologizing as they wrangle a flailing toddler out of the heat. (By the way, there's never a need to apologize for that.) When that happens, I usually smile and say, "I get it. Honestly, I feel the same way he does right now, too."

Because here's the truth:
Even in magical places—even surrounded by churros and castle views—we can break down.
We can be in the middle of goodness and still fall apart.

We love to quote the verse about childlike faith—usually imagining innocent wonder: wide eyes, easy trust, pure belief.

But being a child also means… meltdowns. It means being overwhelmed, out of words, out of strength, and clinging desperately to someone bigger when the world feels too much.

That's us, too.

Joy doesn't mean everything goes according to plan..
Joy doesn't mean life is perfectly calm.
Joy doesn't mean you've got it all together.

Sometimes life throws things at us that hurt.
Sometimes we're overworked, overtired, and just… over it.
Sometimes we don't even know what's wrong—we just know we're not okay.

So what do we do when we hit the wall?

When the magic wears off and the meltdown moves in—can Joy really live there, too?

I think so.

Because what happened next in Tomorrowland said it all.

That little boy was losing it. But then I watched something beautiful happen: his mom gently picked him up. He was still kicking and wailing, but he wrapped his arms around her like a lifeline. He didn't have words—but he had dependence. He held on.

She didn't scold him. She didn't shame him. She simply said,
"Let's go take a nap."
 She carried him in all his mess. And she didn't let go.

And in that moment, I couldn't help but think—this is what God does for us.
He carries us, too—mess and all.

"The eternal God is your refuge, and underneath
are the everlasting arms."
(Deuteronomy 33:27)

Even when we're melting down, His arms never let go.

Remember Elijah under the broom tree? (1 Kings 19:4–8)
He was exhausted. Overwhelmed. Done.
He literally said, "I have had enough, Lord."

And what did God do?
He didn't lecture him.
He didn't tell him to get it together.
He sent an angel.
With a nap. And a snack.
Then another nap. And another snack.

God met Elijah in his meltdown—not with pressure, but with kindness and care.

Sometimes, the holiest thing you can do is rest—and let yourself be held.

And that kind of gentle response?
It's not a one-time thing.
It's the very heart of God toward the overwhelmed.

"The Lord is close to the brokenhearted and saves
those who are crushed in spirit."
(Psalm 34:18)

God doesn't roll His eyes when you fall apart.
He leans in.
He doesn't shame your overwhelm.
He meets you in it.
He doesn't ask you to pull yourself together before He shows up.
He steps right into the mess.

Maybe your meltdown moments aren't signs of failure—
but reminders of your need.

And maybe that's where Joy is found:
Not in holding it all together,
but in knowing that even when you don't...
God still holds you.
Right there.
Right in the middle of it.

> *"Because of the Lord's great love we are not consumed,*
> *for His compassions never fail. They are new every morning."*
> **(Lamentations 3:22–23)**

> *"He tends His flock like a shepherd:*
> *He gathers the lambs in His arms and*
> *carries them close to His heart."*
> **(Isaiah 40:11)**

So give yourself grace.
God already has.

Pause + Ponder

Let these questions guide you into grace—not guilt.

✦ What situations or patterns tend to lead you to emotional burnout?

✦ When was the last time you felt emotionally undone—and how
did you respond?

✦ How do you imagine God responding to you in those moments?

_____

_____

✦ What would it look like to invite Him into the hard emotions—
not just the happy ones?

_____

_____

A BLESSING FOR THE OVERWHELMED:

May you know that even when the magic fades... the Miracle stays.
May you find Joy not in your strength—but in your surrender.
And when you melt down (because we all do)...
May you find yourself held by the gentle, unwavering love of God.

He's not going anywhere.
So hold on tight. Or let go.
Either way... He's got you.

DAY TWO
LIVING IT OUT:
JOY IN THE MELTDOWN

*E*ven in the most magical place on earth, that little boy remind-ed us all: there are moments when we just *lose it*.
And maybe you've been there lately—overwhelmed, exhausted, wondering if you're somehow "failing" for falling apart.

Here's the truth: God isn't asking you to hold it all together. He's inviting you to let Him hold *you*.

So today, we're going to practice surrender.
Not the kind that gives up, but the kind that gives *over*.

You don't have to fix yourself before you come to Him.
You just have to reach out and let Him carry you—mess, tears, chocolate-streaked cheeks and all.

Read

> "The eternal God is your refuge, and
> underneath are the everlasting arms."
> **— Deuteronomy 33:27**

> "The Lord is close to the brokenhearted and saves
> those who are crushed in spirit."
> **— Psalm 34:18**

Reflect

Take a few minutes in a quiet place and ask yourself:

+ Where have I been trying too hard to hold it all together?

+ How has my heart been weary, overwhelmed, or undone lately?

+ What would it look like to let God meet me there—instead of trying to fix it myself?

Write down what comes to mind. No editing, no shame — just honesty.

Respond

Find a simple way to let yourself *be held* today.
Here are a few ideas:

+ Take a walk and pray as if you're just talking to your Father, telling Him everything without filtering it.
+ Lie down and simply rest, breathing deeply and whispering, *"Thank You for holding me."*

Songs for Today

+ *"Lean Back"* — Capital City Music
+ *"You Hold It All Together"* — Maverick City Music

A PRAYER FOR TODAY

Lord, I don't have to hold it all together, because You already hold me. Thank You for catching me when I fall, for carrying me when I can't take another step, for loving me when I'm messy and undone. Remind me that Joy isn't about perfection — it's about being held by You, even here, even now. Amen.

Chapter 4:

JOY IN THE
WILD PLACES

DAY ONE
WHEN THE ROAD IS ROUGH
· ·

When you climb aboard Kilimanjaro Safari, you give up control—and you never quite know what's coming. There's no track, no safety rail, and you don't know the script -just a bumpy road, and whatever comes into view next. That's part of what makes it so thrilling—and a little nerve-wracking.

Maybe that's why it's one of the most popular attractions in the park. Every ride brings something new. You never know exactly what animals you'll see or how close they'll get. It's a wild adventure every time.

Plus, there's always the hope of spotting lions, cheetahs, elephants—and maybe even a bearcat. (Yes, that's a real animal. No, it's not just from a Disney movie.)

One thing you can count on? It's going to be bumpy. Disney designed this ride to feel like a real African safari, and it delivers. The truck jostles over uneven roads, water crossings and wooden bridges, all while giving you front-row seats to some of the most majestic animals on earth. It's convincing—so much so that you forget you're in the middle of Florida.

I remember one particular safari where I was seated next to a family with a young boy who was absolutely lit up with excitement. Every time the truck turned a corner or bounced over a dip, he squealed with delight and pointed out every animal he saw. "There's a giraffe! There's another one!"

At one point, our truck came to a full stop as a tower of giraffes crossed the road in front of us. One of them bent its long neck, inching surprisingly close to our vehicle. The boy's enthusiasm turned into wide-eyed silence. I watched as a look of fear spread across his face and he instinctively reached for his dad's hand.

His dad didn't flinch. He just smiled and held on tight. And after a few minutes of security, the boy relaxed again. By the time we rounded the next corner and spotted a herd of elephants, his excitement returned just as strong.

That moment stuck with me—not just because it was sweet, but because it looked a lot like faith. The shift from delight to fear, then back to peace—all because he knew he wasn't alone.

Life feels a lot like that safari, doesn't it? Bumpy, full of surprises, and sometimes a little too close for comfort.. One moment you're cruising with confidence, and the next you're gripping the sides of the seat wondering what's around the next bend.

But the truth is, we were never meant to go it alone. That's the kind of reassurance I need when life feels like it's veering off course.

Thankfully, God doesn't leave us guessing or navigating alone. He tells us clearly in Deuteronomy 31:6:

> *"Be strong and courageous. Do not be afraid or terrified*
> *because of them, for the Lord your God goes with*
> *you; He will never leave you nor forsake you."*

I don't know about you, but I'm most grateful for God's presence in the unpredictable moments of life. When the road gets rough ahead and you're miles and miles from your nice warm bed... (Okay, I broke out into song again. I'll stop.)

Let's get back on track...when the road gets rough and the fear creeps in, I need to know that He's right there beside me—and He always is.

Isaiah 42:16 paints a beautiful picture of that promise:

> *"I will lead the blind by ways they have not known, along*
> *unfamiliar paths I will guide them; I will turn the darkness*
> *into light before them and make the rough places smooth."*

We don't have to know the whole map. We just need to trust the Guide.

Proverbs 20:24 puts it this way:

> *"The Lord directs our steps, so why try to*
> *understand everything along the way?"*

Sometimes we get caught up trying to make sense of every twist and turn. But faith isn't about understanding the whole route—it's about trusting the One who knows the destination.

Joy doesn't mean the road isn't bumpy. It means knowing who's riding with you. And knowing He's riding with you? That changes everything.

It means trusting that even when the giraffe gets too close, God is still holding your hand. He's not just a guide; He's our peace in the panic, our calm in the chaos, and our strength when the road feels too much.

The truth is, I've tried being my own safari guide. I've grabbed the wheel, thinking I knew the better route. But it always leads to more confusion, more detours, and more unnecessary bumps.

When I let God lead, the road doesn't suddenly become straight and smooth—but it does become purposeful. It becomes guided. And that brings peace I can't manufacture on my own.

You can still be afraid and still choose Joy. You can still be uncertain and still move forward. You can still be in the middle of a wild ride and still trust the One steering.

So if life feels unpredictable right now, you're not alone. Maybe it's time to loosen your grip on the wheel and take His hand instead.

Pause + Ponder

✦ Where do you feel like your life is currently "off-road" or uncertain?

✦ What would it look like to trust God with the steering wheel?

✦ What's one situation where you need to be strong and courageous right now?

✦ Can you name a time in the past where God guided you safely through something unpredictable?

May your courage rise higher than your fears, and may you find Joy in the wild and unexpected turns. And may you never forget—you're not on this safari alone.

A BLESSING FOR THE JOURNEY THROUGH THE WILD

May you feel the steady grip of His hand when the road gets rough.

May your heart stay light even when the path grows heavy.

May you find Joy not in knowing the way, but in trusting the Guide.

When the bumps come and the giraffes get a little *too close*, may you laugh anyway—because you know you're not alone.

And as you navigate the twists and turns ahead, may His peace calm your fears, His presence steady your steps, and His love remind you:

You don't have to steer each wild ride.

You just have to hold on.

DAY TWO
LIVING IT OUT:
JOY IN THE BUMPS

Let's be honest: bumpy roads aren't just part of safari rides—they're part of life.

Sometimes you're cruising along just fine...
...and then come the unexpected detours, the potholes of discouragement, the turns you didn't see coming.

It's easy to assume that if the road is rough, we must've taken a wrong turn. But that's not always true. Sometimes, God leads us *straight into the wilderness*—not to abandon us, but to remind us that He is still near.

The wild places teach us how to trust.

They teach us to let go of needing to see the whole path and instead lean into the One who guides it.

So today, we're going to release our white-knuckle grip on control. We're going to sit in the seat, look around at the beauty (even if it's chaotic), and remember: we are never riding alone.

You can still be rattled... and still be rooted in Joy.

You can still feel uncertain... and still be anchored in peace.

You can still be in the middle of the wilderness... and still know you're held.

Read

"I will lead the blind by ways they have not known,
along unfamiliar paths I will guide them;
I will turn the darkness into light before them
and make the rough places smooth."
— Isaiah 42:16

"The Lord directs our steps,
so why try to understand everything along the way?"
— Proverbs 20:24

Reflect

Take a few deep breaths and ask yourself:

✦ Where in my life do I feel like the road is especially bumpy right now?

✦ What emotions rise up when I don't know what's coming next?

✦ What would it look like to stop trying to steer and start trusting God's direction—even if I can't see the whole map?

Write down what surfaces. Be honest, even if it's messy. Especially if it's messy.

_____

_____

_____

_____

_____

Respond

Practice letting go of the wheel today. Here are a few simple ways:

✦ Take a few minutes in silence. Open your hands and simply say, "Lord, I trust You to guide me."

✦ Go outside and take a walk with no destination in mind. Let it remind you that it's okay not to know every step ahead.

Songs for Today

✦ *"Shepherd"* — Amanda Cook

✦ "Sovereign Over Us" by Aaron Keyes

A PRAYER FOR TODAY

Lord, sometimes the road feels too rough, too uncertain, too wild. But I believe You're with me in it all.
Thank You for being my Guide when I can't see the path ahead.
Thank You for staying steady when I feel shaken.
Help me release control and rest in the truth that You're holding the map—and holding me, too.
Let Joy rise up even on the bumpiest days, because You're with me, always.
Amen.

Chapter 5

SAVORING LIFE'S LITTLE MOMENTS

DAY ONE
JOY IN THE MOMENTS WE ALMOST MISS

· ·

Toy Story Land at Disney's Hollywood Studios brings out all the smiles. Everywhere you look, the details transport you back to childhood playtime—giant board games, Green Army Men, Lincoln Logs, wooden blocks—the list goes on.

One day as I exited Midway Mania, I stopped in front of something I had walked past a hundred times before: a giant wooden airplane model. But this time, I stopped in my tracks. Instantly, memories from summer camp came rushing in—running up and down a big hill with friends, launching those little wooden planes and cheering to see whose would fly the farthest.

Hours of play. Simple Joy. Not a care in the world.

Talk about a flight down memory lane.

That's the thing about Toy Story Land—it isn't just for kids. I love watching everyone soak it all in. The smell of tater tots wafting from Woody's Lunch Box. Dads posing proudly in front of the giant Buzz Lightyear. Moms aiming for high scores on Midway Mania.

The laughter, the squeals, the shared Joy. It's beautiful.

One of my favorite memories happened on Slinky Dog Dash.

Two teenage boys—probably around 15—stood in front of me in line. At first, they looked like your typical "too cool for school" teens, but you could tell they were excited.

The moment Slinky took off, their cool personas disappeared. They laughed. They threw their hands in the air. And best of all, as the coaster neared the end and Wheezy the Penguin began singing "You've Got a Friend in Me," those two boys sang right along—pretending to hold microphones, belting out every word to each other like it was their anthem.

A wooden plane. A photo op with Buzz. The smell of tater tots. A silly roller coaster singalong.

These may not be big moments—but they're beautiful ones. And sometimes, all it takes is a fresh perspective to see it.

Even if it's your very first time noticing. We often chase mountaintop experiences, but God frequently meets us in the small, ordinary ones.

Mountaintops are amazing—but don't miss the Joy that's already surrounding you.

Be present. Pay attention to what God is doing right now in the everyday moments. James 1:17 reminds us, "Every good and perfect gift is from above…"

And Ecclesiastes 3:12–13 tells us,

> *"There is nothing better for people than to be happy and to do good while they live… this is the gift of God."*

Psalm 90:14 adds,

> *"Satisfy us in the morning with your unfailing love, that we may sing for joy and be glad all our days."*

Joy isn't meant to be rare. It's meant to be daily. Good is all around us. Laughter is a gift. Joy is a blessing.

And happiness, in its purest form, is sacred.

Too often, we seek God only in crisis or hardship—but don't forget to find Him in the laughter, in the music, and yes, even in the wonderful smell of tater tots.

Savor the flavor.

Listen for laughter.

Sing even louder.

Spiritual growth isn't always born in fire or flood—sometimes it's found in fries and friendship, in giggles and grace.

Joy isn't only for the valley or the mountaintop—it thrives in the middle. In the ordinary. In the moments we almost miss. It lives in play, in pause, and in presence. This is the Joy of the in-between—the laughter, the shared memories, the goofy, simple, sacred moments.

Let's not miss them.

Pause + Ponder

✦ What are three small things today that made you smile?

✦ Where in your life are you moving too fast to savor the present?

✦ What does it look like to be more present and more playful this week?

✦ What would change if you saw every moment as a gift?

May you find Joy not only in the big wins but also in the small wonders—and especially everywhere in between. May the little moments point your heart toward the God who is with you in all of them.

DAY TWO
LIVING IT OUT:
JOY IN THE ORDINARY

Big moments get all the attention—celebrations, milestones, mountaintop highs.

But Joy? It often slips in quietly, through the side door of our lives.

It's in the way the sun hits the table just right during breakfast.
It's in the goofy text from a friend that makes you snort-laugh.
It's in a song you forgot you loved.
Or the smell of tater tots that instantly makes you feel 10 years old again.

The world tells us we need to chase extraordinary things. But Jesus modeled a life that was deeply present. He noticed people. He lingered at meals. He washed dusty feet. He paused.

When we race through life, we miss the beauty right in front of us.

But when we slow down and pay attention, the ordinary transforms into sacred.
The mundane becomes magical.
The background becomes the blessing.

So today, we practice presence. We live with our eyes open. We don't wait for something "big" to be grateful—we recognize that small is not the opposite of sacred.

It's often where God shows up most.

Let's tune our hearts to Joy—not just in the highlight reel, but in the real life that's happening right now.

Read

"Better one handful with tranquility than two handfuls
with toil and chasing after the wind."
— Ecclesiastes 4:6

"This is the day the Lord has made. We will rejoice and be glad in it."
— Psalm 118:24

Reflect

Take a few quiet minutes and ask yourself:

✦ Where in my day am I rushing past moments that could bring Joy?

✦ What is one simple, often-overlooked part of my routine that I could start seeing as a gift?

✦ When was the last time I let myself *play* or be silly, without worrying how it looked?

Write freely and without pressure—Joy loves honest reflection.

Songs for Today

+ "Goodness of God"— CeCe Winans
+ *"Step By Step"* — Rich Mullins

Respond

Here are a few ways to savor life's little moments today:

+ Pause during a normal part of your day—drinking coffee, folding laundry, standing in line—and silently thank God for that moment.
+ Do something playful just because it brings you delight. (No productivity required.)
+ Text someone a favorite shared memory—remind them (and yourself) of Joy you've already experienced.

A PRAYER FOR TODAY

Lord,
Help me not to miss what's right in front of me.
Teach me to see You in the little things—in the smells, the sounds, the laughter, the quiet.
Thank You for the kind of Joy that doesn't need a stage or spotlight.
Give me eyes to notice, a heart that pauses, and a spirit that delights in Your everyday goodness.
Let my life be filled with holy wonder at the ordinary.
Amen.

Chapter 6

JOY LIKE IT'S YOUR FIRST TIME

DAY ONE
REDISCOVERING AWE
IN THE FAMILIAR

One of my favorite little Disney touches is the celebration buttons they give out when you enter the park gates. You've probably seen them—birthday buttons, anniversary buttons, "I'm Celebrating" buttons, and of course, the bright orange one that says "1st Visit."

There's something about that First Visit button that gets me every time. When I spot someone wearing one, I can't help but smile—and a small part of me wishes I could see the parks through their eyes again. That wide-eyed wonder, the uncontainable excitement, the feeling that *everything* is magical.

I once watched a family over in Tomorrowland—dad, mom, two kids, all wearing their First Visit buttons. The little boy looked at the map and shouted, "Let's go ride Space Mountain!" Without hesitation, the dad said, "Let's go!" like it was the happiest idea in the world. From where we stood, you could see Space Mountain towering in the distance, and the older brother gasped, "This is so incredible!"

It was like watching a commercial come to life.

I've seen that building hundreds—maybe thousands—of times. I've ridden Space Mountain more times than I can count. But seeing their reaction made me realize something: the ride hadn't changed.

I had. The magic was still there—I had just grown used to it. Familiarity dulls the sparkle—even of the most dazzling gifts..

Somewhere along the way, the thrill became familiar. The magic became routine.

That moment stuck with me—because it's not just about Space Mountain. It's about life. It's about how easily we let the extraordinary become ordinary.

I'll catch myself scrolling on my phone while riding the PeopleMover, or breezing past the carefully-crafted queue of Journey of the Little Mermaid, not even noticing the artistry all around me. I've even dozed off during Carousel of Progress (don't judge me—it's air-conditioned). And if I can doze through the story of progress, how often do I drift past the presence of God's amazing grace?

But that family reminded me of something so important: the blessings haven't changed. *I've just stopped noticing them.*

And you know what? We do the same thing with our faith.

The truths that once made us weep—the Grace that saved us, the God who sees us, the cross that rescued us —can quietly fade into background noise. Maybe you remember that first worship song that moved you to tears. Or the moment you truly grasped that you were forgiven. What once felt like a miracle can quietly become just another Sunday.. We believe it, but we don't *feel* it the same way. Not because it's less powerful—but because we've grown used to it.

But first-time faith? That's where Joy lives. In the awe. In the wonder. In the remembering that God's love should never feel "normal." It should take our breath away.

In Revelation 2:4-5, Jesus says,

> *"You have forsaken the love you had at first. Consider how f ar you have fallen! Repent and do the things you did at first."*

It's His gentle way of saying, "Come back. Remember. Fall in love with Me all over again."

Joy grows best in hearts that keep rediscovering wonder. When we pause long enough to see familiar blessings with fresh eyes—everything changes.

So here's your invitation: slow down. Look around. Don't just walk past the good stuff. Be amazed again. Live like it's your first visit.

Because the wonder isn't gone—you've just stopped looking.

Let's get back to noticing.

Grab your journal and take time to rediscover what might have become familiar.

Pause + Ponder

✦ When was a time your faith felt full of wonder?

✦ Write down 40 blessings that you may have allowed to become mundane.

✦ Where might God be inviting you to notice Him with fresh eyes?

✦ What would change if you lived today like it was your very first "visit"?

PRAYER:

May your eyes be opened to the wonder that's been with you all along.

May the familiar become fresh, and the blessings you once over-looked shine bright again.

May your heart return to its first love—the God who has never stopped loving you.

And as you walk through this day, may you do so with first-time faith—

full of Joy, full of wonder, full of wide-eyed trust.

May today feel like your very first visit—

and may the awe never wear off.

DAY TWO
LIVING IT OUT:
REDISCOVERING WONDER

It's easy to lose the sparkle when we've seen something a hundred times.
The ride is still thrilling. The view is still beautiful.
But our eyes?
They've grown used to it.

Familiarity doesn't just dull the magic—it can dampen our Joy.
And that's true not just at Disney… but in our faith.

Maybe you remember what it felt like to believe for the first time.
To hear that you were fully forgiven.
To realize you were truly known and completely loved.
To feel worship stir something deep in your soul.

Somewhere along the way, that passion may have settled into something… quieter.
Less sparkly. More routine.

But here's the beautiful truth: the Gospel hasn't changed. God hasn't moved.
The blessings are still breathtaking—if we'll just *notice* them again.

Revelation 2:4 doesn't shame us—it *invites* us.
"Come back," Jesus says. "Remember. Fall in love all over again."

So today, we slow down.
We pay attention.
We walk like it's our first visit again.

And as we do, we rediscover the Joy that never actually left—it was just waiting to be seen again.

Read

> *"You have forsaken the love you had at first.*
> *Consider how far you have fallen! Repent and do the things you did at first."*
> **— Revelation 2:4–5**

> *"Restore to me the joy of your salvation and grant me a willing spirit,*
> *to sustain me."*
> **— Psalm 51:12**

Reflect

Take time to quietly reflect:

✦ What parts of your faith have become so familiar that you've stopped really seeing them?

✦ When was the last time you felt wide-eyed wonder at God's love?

✦ What blessings in your life have you been walking past without noticing?

Write freely. Let God awaken awe in the places you've grown numb.

_____

_____

_____

Respond

Here are a few ways to bring back "first-time faith" today:

✦ Worship like it's the first time. Play that worship song that once brought you to tears and let yourself feel it again.

✦ Notice the details. Whether you're at the grocery store, the park, or your kitchen sink—ask God to help you see the beauty that's already there.

✦ Say thank you for 10 small things you usually take for granted—food, friends, forgiveness. Speak it out loud. Let gratitude wake up your heart.

Songs for Today

✦ *"How Great Thou Art"* — Garett & Kate

✦ *"Wonderful Cross"* — Chris Tomlin & Matt Redman

A PRAYER FOR TODAY

Lord,
I confess that I've grown used to some of the most amazing things—Your love, Your grace, Your presence.
I don't want to just go through the motions.
I want to see You again, like it's the first time.
Give me fresh eyes to see old blessings.
Help me slow down long enough to remember what once left me in awe.
Restore to me the Joy of my salvation.
I want to live today full of wonder—full of worship—full of You.
Amen.

LIVING ON PURPOSE

DAY ONE
WHAT IF YOU PLANNED
LIFE LIKE A DISNEY
VACATION?

*Y*ou've seen it—someone posts their Walt Disney World countdown with over 300 days to go and they're already deep in planning mode: where to eat, what to wear, how to get from the airport to the resort, and which snacks are absolutely non-negotiable.

I mean—they plan. We're talking spreadsheets, color-coded calendars, park reservations, matching T-shirts, snack goals, parade strategy, and Genie+ bookings timed to the minute. They've watched all the YouTube videos, read every blog post, joined multiple Facebook groups, and maybe even practiced rope-dropping in their driveway.

Even if they don't want to do all the planning themselves, they hire a Disney Travel Planner to take care of it all (a wise move if you ask me). But one way or another, the details are set.

I recently saw a family checking into Port Orleans Riverside and a Mom pulled out her notebook that looked thicker than any book in the Beast's library!

Before moving to Disney, I was the same way. I'd plan out my days, my meals, the rides I wanted to ride. I'd imagine myself soaring on Soarin', climbing Everest, and yes—I could practically taste the churro as I mapped it all out.

All that... for one magical week.

And yet—most of us don't plan our actual lives that way.

We'll spend a year planning a vacation—but barely five minutes planning for the week ahead. We'll dream about Disney—but forget to dream about our own lives.

That realization hit me—and it's been echoing in my heart ever since. Because maybe Joy doesn't come from magical experiences at all—maybe it comes, in part, from meaningful, intentional living.

When we coast through life on autopilot, the days blur. We wake up, scroll, work, eat, sleep, repeat. But what if we approached our lives with the same thoughtfulness and purpose we give to a Disney itinerary?

What if we actually designed our days instead of just surviving them?

Living with intention doesn't mean packing your schedule—it means filling your days with purpose. Margin matters. Rest matters. We need breathing room. Living on purpose means choosing what matters most—and doing it on purpose.

Jesus lived this way. He pulled away to rest. He spent time with people. He walked with clarity, grace, and purpose. Psalm 90:12 puts it beautifully:

> *"Teach us to number our days, that we may gain a heart of wisdom."*

We don't control how many days we get—but we do choose how we spend them.

You're not here by accident. God created you on purpose, for a purpose. He's not calling you to hustle harder—but to live more intentionally.

There is deep Joy in knowing your days are shaped by what truly matters. When your calendar reflects your calling. When you start saying "yes" to the things that matter—and "no" to the distractions that don't.

Proverbs 16:3 says,

> *"Commit to the Lord whatever you do, and He will establish your plans."*
> *And Ephesians 2:10 reminds us, "For we are God's handiwork, created in*
> *Christ Jesus to do good works, which God prepared in advance for us to do."*

Have you ever noticed how every Cast Member at Disney has a specific role to play? Each one contributes something unique to the magic of the experience. God's Kingdom works the same way—He's given you a role, too. A purpose. A calling. And you bring something to His story that no one else can.

There's something deeply Joy-filled about living that out.

So no, I'm not saying your life needs to be planned out to the second like a Disney day. (Although matching shirts are still encouraged.) But maybe start small:

Block out time to rest. Create space for prayer. Schedule time to be in the Word. Use your gifts. Look for ways to bless the world around you. Write down your dreams. Reclaim your mornings. Plan a walk with a friend. Say "yes" to what brings life. Say "no" to what drains it.

Joy doesn't just appear—it's cultivated in the quiet choices. One intentional moment at a time.

Pause + Ponder

✦ What are some areas of your life that currently feel unplanned or aimless?

✦ What would it look like to "live on purpose" in this next season?

✦ Are there activities or habits on your calendar that bring you more stress than Joy?

✦ What are five small but meaningful things you could schedule this week to make space for more Joy?

PRAYER:

May your days be shaped by purpose, not pressure.

May you number your days—not to rush through them, but to treasure each one.

May your schedule reflect the things that draw you closer to God and to the people you love.

And may your life—every ordinary Tuesday and every magical moment—be filled with the kind of intentional Joy you'd pack for the trip of a lifetime.

You were made for this journey.

Live it well.

Live it on purpose.

DAY TWO
LIVING IT OUT:
PLANNING FOR JOY

If we're honest, most of us have put more time into planning a Disney day than we have into planning how we want to live the next season of our lives.

And yet, Joy doesn't just happen by accident.
It's nurtured.
It's cultivated.
It's chosen.

Living with intention doesn't mean filling every hour. It means filling your life with purpose.

When you create margin for what matters—time with God, rest, laughter, calling, connection—you open the door for Joy to settle in and stay awhile.

Jesus modeled this beautifully. He knew His mission, yet He still paused to pray, retreated to rest, and made space to eat with friends. He lived with purpose, not pressure.

Psalm 90:12 says,

"Teach us to number our days, that we may gain a heart of wisdom."
That's not a call to hustle—it's a call to treasure the time we've been given and spend it wisely, intentionally, and meaningfully.

So what would it look like to plan *for* Joy this week?

Not just the tasks that need doing—but the moments that give life.
Not just what's urgent—but what's truly important.
What if your calendar reflected the kind of life you *want* to live?

This week, let's plan with purpose.
Let's schedule what matters.
Let's be intentional about delight.
Let's reclaim the Joy that's waiting in the margins.

Read

> *"Commit to the Lord whatever you do, and He will establish your plans."*
> **— Proverbs 16:3**

> *"For we are God's handiwork, created in Christ Jesus to do good works, which God prepared in advance for us to do."*
> **— Ephesians 2:10**

Reflect

Take a moment to ask yourself:

✦ What parts of my life feel like they're just on autopilot?

✦ Where do I need to create more space for rest, worship, connection, or calling?

✦ What's one area where I can stop reacting—and start planning with purpose?

Write it down. Let God guide you as you map out the days ahead.

Respond

Try one of these simple, intentional practices this week:

✦ Schedule your rest. Literally block time in your calendar to pause, pray, or take a breath.

✦ Make a mini "Joy plan." List 3 things that bring you life (big or small), and add them to your week like you would any important appointment.

✦ Choose one life-giving "yes" and one stress-reducing "no." Let your priorities shape your calendar—not just your to-do list.

Songs for Today

✦ *"If I Stand"* — Rich Mullins

✦ *"Make Room"* — Community Music / Elyssa Smith

A PRAYER FOR TODAY

Lord,
Teach me to number my days, not to rush through them, but to cherish them.
Show me how to live with intention—how to create space for what brings You glory and brings me life.

Help me say yes to the things that matter, and no to what distracts me.
I don't want to drift—I want to walk with purpose.
So today, I commit my time to You.
Shape my schedule. Shape my heart.
And let Joy fill the spaces I've made for You.
And in the places I hold on for control - remind me that those are the spaces where I need you most.
Amen.

◇◇◇◇◇◇◇◇◇◇◇◇◇◇ *Chapter 8:* ◇◇◇◇◇◇◇◇◇◇◇◇◇◇

JUST KEEP JUMPING

DAY ONE
WHAT A LITTLE GIRL
AT TYPHOON LAGOON
TAUGHT ME ABOUT TRUST

She couldn't have been more than four—but in that moment, she was fearless.

She stepped back from the edge of the pool, took a running start, locked eyes with her dad—and jumped. Arms flailing. Hair flying. Joy bursting from her face. She landed with a splash right into his waiting arms, erupting in laughter and the kind of squeals only pure delight can produce.

Her dad carried her back to the edge—and she leapt again, full of squeals and sparkle. No hesitation. No fear. Just a continual game of "Catch me, Daddy!"

She never asked if he was ready.
She didn't look around for permission.
She just trusted.

That simple, childlike trust? It was beautiful to watch.

Tucked in a corner of Disney's Typhoon Lagoon—where the Crush 'n' Gusher empties into a wading pool—this little pocket of magic was unfolding. Palm trees swayed, the sun sparkled on the water, and a dad and his daughter made a memory he will never forget.

And as I watched her leap again and again—without a flicker of doubt—I couldn't help but wonder:

Isn't this what faith is supposed to look like?

Faith isn't just believing God exists—it's living like He can be trusted.
It's running toward Him, full speed.
It's jumping without hesitation.
It's trusting that His arms will be there—again and again and again.

And yet... most of us don't jump like that.

Even though we've experienced God's faithfulness time and time again, we hesitate. We overthink. We question.
We try to calculate risk before we leap.

But what if faith looked more like that little girl's?
What if it was less about logic and more about love—less about certainty and more about trust?

That kind of faith moves mountains.
That kind of trust brings Joy.

We often call on faith when we're going through our own typhoons—when the waters rise, when life feels overwhelming.

Isaiah 43:2 says,

> *"When you pass through the waters, I will be with you."*

Not if—when.
The storms are part of life. But so is God's presence.

Peter's leap of faith? He actually walked on water—eyes locked on Jesus, steps steady.

Then... distraction. Fear.

The wind rose. The waves swelled.

He began to sink.

"Lord, save me!" he cried.

And Jesus?

Immediately—He reached out His hand and caught him.

That's my kind of faith journey right there.
Some bold steps. Some sinking moments.
A whole lot of grace in between.

Honestly, Peter feels like the poster child for my faith.
I know God's got me—but distractions still get loud.
I start sinking... and every time, He's still there. Hand out. Arms open. Ready to catch.

It's the faith of that little girl that I long for:
Eyes locked on the Father.
Feet pounding with purpose.
A heart that just keeps jumping.

Because here's the truth:
Joy doesn't come from calm waters.

Joy comes from knowing—without a doubt—Who's already in the water with you.

Even when the waves rise.
Even when you're unsure.
Even when you've been hurt before—He is there.

Your faith doesn't have to be perfect.
Your leap doesn't have to be graceful.
But every time you jump, you build deeper trust in God, who always catches.

You're not leaping alone.
The One who calls you to jump is already in the water—arms open, steady and strong.

So whether you're standing at the edge or mid-air in faith... Just keep jumping.

Pause + Ponder

Let these questions guide your heart into deeper trust:

✦ What keeps you from "jumping" into God's arms with full trust?

✦ When was the last time you stepped out in faith—and what happened?

✦ What would it look like to trust God more freely, like a child?

✦ In what area of your life do you feel God saying, "Jump—I've got you"?

A BLESSING FOR THE ONE WHO DARES TO JUMP

May you run to the edge and leap without hesitation—
Not because life is easy, but because your Father is faithful.
May your heart learn to trust again—fully, freely, fearlessly.
And when the waves rise...
May you feel His arms already there.

DAY TWO
LIVING IT OUT: TRUST
WITHOUT HESITATION
· · · · · · · · · · · · · · · · · · · ·

Trust doesn't always look polished.
Sometimes it's messy, loud, wet, and full of wild squeals.
Sometimes it looks like a four-year-old launching herself into her father's arms—again and again and again.

That's the kind of trust God invites us into.

Not cautious. Not over-analyzed.
But wide-eyed. Open-hearted.
Certain of who's waiting on the other side of the leap.

And yet, most of us hesitate.

We fear the fall. We overthink the jump. We wonder, "Will He really catch me this time?"

But He always does.

Isaiah 43:2 doesn't say,

> *"If you pass through the waters…"*
> *It says when. Storms are a given—but so is His presence.*

Faith doesn't eliminate fear—it just chooses to jump anyway.
It's saying, "I don't know how this ends, but I know Who's catching me."

The little girl at Typhoon Lagoon didn't jump once and call it done. She kept leaping—again and again—each time building more joy, more laughter, and more trust.

You can, too.

Even if you've been disappointed before.
Even if your last leap didn't look the way you hoped.
Even if the waves are high today.

Joy doesn't come from knowing the outcome.
Joy comes from knowing the One who's waiting to catch you.

So today, practice the jump.
Even if your feet barely leave the ground.
Even if your heart's not fully there yet.

Because trust grows with every leap.
And grace is always waiting in the splash.

Read

"When you pass through the waters, I will be with you..."
—Isaiah 43:2

*"Immediately Jesus reached out His hand and caught him.
'You of little faith,' He said, 'why did you doubt?'"*
—Matthew 14:31

Reflect

Take some quiet time to consider:

✦ What has made you hesitate to trust God fully in this season?

+ Can you remember a time when you did take a leap of faith—and He caught you?

+ Where might God be asking you to step out, even if you feel uncertain?

Be honest. Write it down. Even fear can lead you into deeper faith.

Respond

Simple ways to build trust today:

+ Pray with your hands open. Literally open your palms and say, "God, I trust You with this..." and name what you're holding back.
+ Take one small leap. Call someone. Apply for the thing. Say yes. Or say no. Whatever "jump" God is nudging you toward—do it today.
+ Remember your rescue. Journal a time when God came through for you. Let it remind you that He's faithful still.

Songs for Today

+ "Walk by Faith" — Jeremy Camp
+ "Oceans (Where Feet May Fail)" — Hillsong UNITED

A PRAYER FOR TODAY

Father,

You've caught me before—and You'll catch me again.

Still, I confess that I hesitate. I overthink. I get scared.

Help me trust You like that little girl trusted her dad—without doubt, without delay.

Teach me to jump—again and again—into Your arms of grace.

Let my faith grow not from perfection, but from persistence.

And let Joy rise up with every leap.

Because I know You're always there.

Amen.

Chapter 9

WAITING AT FLIGHT OF PASSAGE

DAY ONE

WHAT THE FLIGHT OF PASSAGE QUEUE CAN TEACH US ABOUT PATIENCE

It's 7:58 a.m. at Disney's Animal Kingdom.

The crowd? Buzzing like a swarm of caffeinated bees. The mission? Get to Flight of Passage before that wait time hits triple digits.

As soon as the rope drops, the crowd surges forward like the Daytona 500—people jockeying for position, weaving through the lush walkways of Pandora, all heading to the same destination.

Have you ever waited in the standby queue for Flight of Passage? It's one of the longest—and most talked-about—wait times at Walt Disney World.

Lines at Disney are fascinating. They're a strange mix of emotions: excitement, impatience, boredom, curiosity. Some guests scroll their phones. Others play games. Kids melt down. Strangers strike up conversations. And every so often, you overhear a comment you'll remember all day.

The Flight of Passage queue, in particular, is long, winding, and beautifully immersive.

Towering mountains. Cascading waterfalls. Glowing bioluminescent plants. The hum of unseen creatures all around you.

It's not just a line—it's a story being told.

And that's when it hit me:
This line?
It feels a lot like life.

Even surrounded by beauty... you're still just standing.
Feet aching. Patience stretching.
The early excitement fades. Enthusiasm dims. Tension quietly builds.

We have dreams. Desires. Destinations in our hearts.
But so often, we find ourselves in the in-between—in the waiting.

We pray. We hope. We believe.
And still, nothing seems to move.

Waiting can feel like being stuck.
Like life is passing you by while you stand still.

In those seasons, I sound like a child three minutes into the queue:
"Are we there yet? How much longer?"

But what if the waiting isn't wasted?
What if God is doing some of His most important work in the line?

I remember once complaining to my mom that something was taking forever, and she replied,
"It builds character."
To which I rolled my eyes and said, "I don't want character—I want it to happen."

(Spoiler alert: I didn't get what I wanted. But I did get a lesson in character.)

And now? I'm learning that God doesn't use waiting to frustrate us.
He uses it to form us.

Waiting teaches dependence.
It deepens perspective.
It reshapes our trust.
It re-centers our hope.

Looking back, I can almost always trace God's hand through the wait.
Even when I couldn't see it at the time, I can now say, "Oh... He was there."
He was working. He never left.

Isaiah 40:31 promises:

> *"But those who wait on the Lord shall renew their strength..."*

And Lamentations 3:25–26 reminds us:

> *"The Lord is good to those who wait for Him...*
> *It is good to wait quietly for the salvation of the Lord."*

This kind of waiting isn't passive.
It's not punishment.
It's preparation.

There's a difference between waiting for God and waiting with God.
One feels like you're standing alone in a never-ending line.
The other feels like you've got a hand to hold the whole way through.

With God, waiting becomes holy ground.
It's where He cultivates resilience, clears out distractions, and anchors us in what truly matters.

By the time you finally step onto the ride—whether that's a breakthrough, a long-awaited answer, or the next chapter of your story—it means more.
Because you walked through the waiting.
And you were changed in the line.

Maybe Joy works like that, too.

Joy isn't found in skipping the line.
There's no FastPass or Lightning Lane.
Joy is found in recognizing that—even in the slow, winding, unseen seasons—God is already there.
Joy is knowing He's not just preparing the way... He's preparing you.

So if you find yourself in a season of waiting, hold on to this:

The delay doesn't mean denial.
The wait doesn't mean you've been forgotten.
It means something worth experiencing is ahead.
Trust the One who knows exactly where this line is going.

And when the time finally comes and the doors open...
You step into something breathtaking.
And you realize:
It wasn't just about the ride.
It was about who you became in the line.

Pause + Ponder

Let these questions guide your heart in the waiting:

+ What would trusting God with Joy look like in the middle of wait?

+ How does waiting make you feel—hopeful, anxious, frustrated?

✦ Can you look back at a time when the wait actually prepared you for what was ahead?

✦ What might God be forming in you right now through this delay?

A BLESSING FOR THE WAITING HEART

May you find strength in the waiting—
and Joy in the not-yet.
May you remember that delays aren't detours—
they're divine preparation.
And when the line feels too long,
may you trust that the One who called you
is already preparing something worth the wait.

DAY TWO
LIVING IT OUT:
JOY IN THE WAITING

Waiting rarely feels like holy ground.
It feels slow.
Frustrating.
Quiet.
Still.

And yet... God does some of His deepest, most transformative work in the in-between.

We live in a world that tries to skip the line.
We crave speed. We worship efficiency. We want the shortcut.
But there's no Lightning Lane for spiritual growth.

The standby line—the long, winding, seemingly never-ending wait—is where trust is built.

It's in the waiting where we learn to stop grasping for control.
It's in the waiting where we let go of our timeline and lean into His.

Lamentations 3:26 says,

"It is good to wait quietly for the salvation of the Lord."

Not just bearable.
Good.

Not because the wait itself feels good—but because God meets us there.

He isn't just the God who answers prayers.
He's the God who walks with us between them.

The Flight of Passage queue winds through beauty, story, and intentional design—even when we're too focused on the wait time to see it.
Life's like that, too.

So today, if you're stuck in a season that feels stalled or slow—what if it's not a setback?

What if it's a sacred pause?

God isn't withholding Joy from you.
He's cultivating it in the quiet.

You're not forgotten.
You're being formed.

Read

> *"But those who wait on the Lord shall renew their strength;*
> *they shall mount up with wings like eagles,*
> *they shall run and not be weary,*
> *they shall walk and not faint."*
> **— Isaiah 40:31**

> *"The Lord is good to those who wait for Him,*
> *to the soul who seeks Him."*
> **— Lamentations 3:25**

Reflect

Take a few moments to journal and reflect:

✦ Where in your life are you waiting right now?

✦ How have you been viewing that season—through frustration or faith?

✦ What might God be growing in you while you wait?

Write freely, and invite God to reframe how you see the line.

Respond

Waiting doesn't have to be passive. Here are a few ways to make space for Joy in the in-between:

✦ Create a "waiting prayer." Each time you feel the urge to complain or worry, offer a simple prayer: "Lord, I trust You in this delay."

✦ Start a "God was there" list. Look back on past waiting seasons and jot down how God came through. Let past faithfulness fuel present hope.

✦ Encourage someone else who's waiting. A text, a card, a kind word—it doesn't just lift them up, it reminds you that waiting is universal... and God is faithful to all.

Songs for Today

✦ "Take Courage" — Kristene DiMarco / Bethel Music

✦ "Even If" — MercyMe

A PRAYER FOR TODAY

Lord,
Waiting is hard.
But I know You are with me in the stillness.
Help me resist the urge to rush through this moment.
Teach me to trust Your timing more than my own agenda.
Form my heart in the pause.
Let Joy take root—even when I don't see the full picture yet.
You are good in the waiting.
You are near in the delay.
And I believe what You have ahead is worth it.
Amen.

Chapter 10

FIREWORKS & FAITHFULNESS

DAY ONE
WHAT HAPPILY EVER AFTER
CAN TEACH US

· · · · · · · · · · · · · · · · · ·

A day at Magic Kingdom brings it all—laughter, magic, thrills, and sometimes... complete exhaustion.
There's something about that park that makes you feel everything.

You start the morning with high hopes and pixie dust energy. You plan. You rush. You ride. You cry (happy tears, usually).
But by the end of the day?

Your feet ache. The kids are cranky. You're questioning every life choice that led to booking that 8:15 p.m. Mobile Order.

But still—you stay. You wait. You hold your spot in front of Cinderella Castle.

And then... the lights dim.

The music begins. A hush falls over the crowd.

And suddenly, the night sky erupts in color.

The fireworks begin.

You feel the rumble in your chest. You see faces lit up by color. You hear someone gasp beside you—and in that moment, it's like the whole park breathes in wonder together.

And just like that—it's all worth it.

The tired legs. The long waits. The Lightning Lanes you missed. The meltdowns—and the moments that didn't make it on social media.

Somehow, the fireworks redeem it all.

No, they don't erase the hard parts of the day...
But they reframe them.
They remind you there was beauty in the chaos.
They send you home with your heart full again.

It's the kind of moment that fills you with a quiet Joy—not because everything went perfectly, but because something deeper broke through.

And standing there, watching it all unfold—it hit me:

This is what God's faithfulness feels like.

It's that same quiet awe—the moment you realize He's been there all along. Steady. Sure. Showing up just when your heart needed it most.

The Sky Isn't Always Bright

Life isn't one big Disney day.
Sometimes, it's more blisters than balloons.
More tears than churros.

And some days don't end in celebration... they end in collapse.

But that's exactly where God meets us.

Not just in the mountaintop moments.
But in the tired aftermath.
When we're worn down and worn out.
When we've got nothing left.

That's when His grace breaks through the dark.

Why Fireworks Matter

The nighttime spectaculars at Disney aren't just tradition—they're intentional.

They're the closing chapter. The final note.
The thing that sends you home with wonder in your heart.

The music, the visuals, the light bursting into the sky—they aren't just entertainment.
They're emotional. They're redemptive.

And that's what God's faithfulness does, too.

It lights up even the darkest sky.
It reminds us the day wasn't wasted.
That even in the mess—He was working.

And when the time is right...
He lifts our eyes.
And lets us see it.

> *"Weeping may endure for a night, but Joy comes in the morning."*
> **—Psalm 30:5**

> *"Because of the Lord's great love we are not consumed...*
> *His mercies are new every morning."*
> **—Lamentations 3:22–23**

Happily Ever After - the show name itself doesn't promise everything goes perfectly—but it does remind you the ending isn't over yet.

When You Feel Like Leaving Early

Here's the thing about fireworks:

You have to stay long enough to see them.

You can't assume they're not coming.
You can't give up and walk away early.

Sometimes you wait in discomfort.
Sometimes you're squished in a crowd.
Sometimes you've got a child asleep on your shoulder.
But still—you stay.

Because when it happens? It's breathtaking.

What if that's also true of God?

What if He's working on something spectacular in your story...
But you're still in the waiting part?

Don't leave early.

Wait for the beauty.
Wait for the breakthrough.

That's where Joy shows up—not in perfection, but in trust. The
deep-down knowing that God is still writing something beautiful.

Pause + Ponder

Let these questions guide your reflection:

✦ What moments in your life felt dark—but were later filled with
  light?

✦ How has God shown up at the "end of the day" for you—after
  the hard part?

✦ Are there areas where you need to wait for the fireworks instead of walking away early?

_____

_____

✦ What's something you're grateful for now that you couldn't see clearly in the moment?

_____

_____

A BLESSING FOR THE ONES STILL WAITING FOR LIGHT

May you stay long enough to see the sky break open with promise.
May you believe that even in your longest night, God is still working.
And when the first light bursts into view,
may your heart remember:

He was always there.
You were never alone.
And your story is still unfolding…
Beautifully.

DAY TWO
LIVING IT OUT: WAITING
FOR THE FIREWORKS

By the end of a Magic Kingdom day, you're not exactly floating on a pixie-dusted cloud.
You're tired. Cranky. Sore.
And if one more child asks for a snack, you might just lose it.

But then... the lights go down.
The music starts.
And the night sky explodes with color.

Something shifts. The day reframes.
And suddenly, it was all worth it.

Life's like that, too.

Some days leave you blistered and battle-worn.
Some seasons feel more meltdown than magic.
You question if you're doing anything right. You wonder where God went.

But He's still there.

And just like the fireworks—His faithfulness has a way of showing up when you need it most.

The truth is:
God's goodness isn't always loud.
It doesn't always follow your timeline.
It doesn't always look like what you pictured.

But it's always on time.
And when you stay long enough to see it—it takes your breath away.

Psalm 30:5 says, "Weeping may endure for a night, but Joy comes in the morning."
But you have to wait for the morning.
You have to stay through the dark.
You have to hold your spot even when the crowd presses in and your arms are tired from carrying what you weren't meant to carry alone.

Don't walk away early.
Don't quit on the edge of breakthrough.
The light is coming.

And when it comes—it will be worth the wait.

Read

"Weeping may endure for a night,
but Joy comes in the morning."
— Psalm 30:5

"Because of the Lord's great love we are not consumed,
for His compassions never fail. They are new every
morning; great is Your faithfulness."
— Lamentations 3:22–23

Reflect

Take a few quiet moments to reflect or journal:

✦ Where in your life are you tempted to "leave early" right now?

+ Can you remember a time when you stuck it out and saw God's faithfulness in the end?

+ What would it look like to stay present—hopeful—even when you don't see the light yet?

Let the memories of His past faithfulness strengthen your current trust.

Respond

Here are a few intentional ways to practice staying for the "fireworks":

+ Light a candle during prayer time. Let the flicker remind you that even a small light breaks darkness—and that God always shows up.
+ Make a "midnight-to-morning" list. Reflect on seasons where things felt hopeless, and note how God eventually moved. Revisit it when you're in the dark again.
+ Encourage someone else to stay. Text or call a friend who's struggling. Tell them they're not alone. Often, Joy multiplies when we remind others it's still coming.

Songs for Today

+ "Faithful Now" — Vertical Worship
+ "Do It Again" – Elevation Worship

A PRAYER FOR TODAY

Lord,
I'm tired. I've been standing in the dark for a while.
But I'm choosing to stay.
Not because I feel strong—but because I trust that You are.
Remind me that the waiting isn't wasted.
Hold me steady until the sky breaks open again.
And when it does, let me see Your faithfulness with fresh eyes.
You are the light in the dark.
You are the color in my story.
And even when I can't see it—I believe the fireworks are coming.
Amen.

Chapter 11

JOY IN EVERY FRAME

DAY ONE
WHAT DISNEY RIDE PHOTOS REVEAL ABOUT HOW GOD SEES US

One of the most fun—and occasionally cringe-worthy—parts of a Disney trip? The PhotoPass experience.

There are photographers all over the parks capturing magical moments you can pose for—smiles in front of the castle, staged jumps, family hugs and the ever-so-popular Magic Shots. You wait your turn, strike your best pose, and almost instantly the perfect memory pops into your app.

But then... there are the ride photos.

Disney has strategically placed cameras on several attractions to catch you mid-scream, mid-laugh, or mid-"What just happened?" Unless you know exactly where the camera is, you're caught mid-wild.

Take Space Mountain for instance.

Now, I love to pose for ride photos. I've ridden Space Mountain more times than I can count, and I usually know exactly when to flash a goofy face or flex like I'm on a billboard. But one time, I got it totally wrong. I turned left to pose, just as the ride turned right. I realized my mistake too late and whipped my head around just as the camera snapped.

The result?
A photo that looked less "space hero" and more "confused potato mid-rollercoaster."

A few strangers behind us saw it pop up and actually laughed out loud—and honestly, I couldn't blame them. It was ridiculous. But in a weird way, it was also my favorite photo from the whole day.

Awkward. Hilarious. Completely real.

But that blurry, wild, unflattering ride photo? It made me think... this is how I show up with God sometimes.

I want Him to see me at my best.
The filtered version.
The posed moments.
The "Sunday Best" version of me with my faith polished and smile practiced.

But God doesn't work off our highlight reels.
He sees us like those ride photos: real, raw, unfiltered.

And here's the beautiful thing—
He doesn't cringe.
He doesn't edit.
He doesn't delete.

He sees the whole you—every expression, every emotion, every frame—and He still calls you beloved. Not because the picture is perfect, but because you are His.

"The Lord does not look at the things people look at...
the Lord looks at the heart."
—1 Samuel 16:7

"You have searched me, Lord, and you know me...
you perceive my thoughts from afar."
—Psalm 139:1–2

I don't know about you, but there are parts of my life I'd rather keep out of the frame.
Mistakes. Regrets. The thoughts I wouldn't post or even admit.
There's a quiet pressure to appear put-together—even before God.

But He already knows. And He loves us right there.

The world teaches us to polish, edit, and filter - so we feel liked, accepted, worthy. But God doesn't love the version you curate. He loves the one He created.

You don't need to filter your faith for it to be beautiful.
You don't have to perform your way into God's affection.
You are not just accepted—you are adored.

Imagine God having a gallery of your life—every photo, every reel, even the ones you'd rather forget.

He doesn't just keep the posed shots.
He treasures the whole slideshow.
The blurry ones. The blinking ones. The vulnerable ones.

Because they're yours.
And you're His.

Joy comes when we stop trying to pose and start letting ourselves be seen—fully, freely, honestly.
That's where intimacy with God begins.
And that's where lasting confidence grows.

You don't have to pose for God.
He already sees you.
And He already loves you.

Even when you're facing the wrong direction and making a con-fused-potato face on Space Mountain... He sees you. And He still smiles.

Joy doesn't come from the perfect photo - it comes from knowing you're already loved in every frame.

And hey - if God's got a gallery of your life, maybe that Space Mountain pic is framed in gold.

Pause + Ponder

Let these questions invite deeper reflection:

+ When have you felt "caught" in a raw or unfiltered moment—how did God meet you there?

+ What do you try to hide or clean up before you come to God?

+ How might your relationship with Him deepen if you lived as someone already fully loved?

+ If God framed a photo of your faith journey, what would it look like today?

A BLESSING FOR THE ONE STILL LEARNING TO LOVE EVERY FRAME

May you know you are seen completely -
and still completely loved.
May you stop hiding the moments you'd rather crop out-
because God already calls them beautiful.
And when you're tempted to pose or perform,
may you remember: the real you is already known...
and already cherished.

DAY TWO
LIVING IT OUT: FULLY SEEN, FULLY LOVED

If you've ever been caught in a ride photo with your eyes shut, your hair flying, and your face doing something... unexplainable—you know the feeling: That can't be what I really look like... right?

But that's the truth about unfiltered moments.
They're real.
They're messy.
They're honest.
And often, they're the ones God cherishes most.

The world teaches us to pose.
To filter.
To curate.
To present the best version of ourselves—even in our faith.

But God isn't drawn to your highlight reel.
He's not waiting for the right angle or lighting.
He sees it all—and loves you in all of it.

Psalm 139 reminds us that God searches us and knows us.
Not just our plans, but our thoughts.
Not just our prayers, but our pauses.
He sees every frame—even the ones we'd delete—and He still calls us beloved.

There's freedom in being fully known.
There's Joy in realizing you don't have to perform for affection or

polish your faith before you come close.
You just have to show up—honestly, imperfectly, completely.

So today, practice being seen.
Take off the filters.
Let God meet you in the middle of the ride—mid-scream, mid-question, mid-"What just happened?"

Because He's not cringing.
He's smiling.
And He's already framed the moment.

Read

"The Lord does not look at the things people look at. People look at the outward appearance, but the Lord looks at the heart."
—1 Samuel 16:7

"You have searched me, Lord, and you know me...
you are familiar with all my ways."
— Psalm 139:1, 3b

Reflect

Use these questions to guide your journaling and quiet time:

✦ Where do you feel tempted to "pose" in your relationship with God?

✦ How would your faith shift if you lived like someone already fully accepted?

✦ What would change if you believed God delights in the real you—not the polished version?

Be honest. God already sees it all. This is just your invitation to see it, too.

Respond

Try one or more of these ways to rest in God's love for the unfiltered you:

✦ Pray unfiltered. Skip the polished phrases. Speak from the heart—messy, real, and raw.

✦ Look through old photos. Pick one where you didn't look "perfect," and ask God to show you how He sees you in it—with delight, not critique.

✦ Write a note to yourself. Begin with "God sees me…" and list five things He knows about you—and still loves.

Songs for Today

✦ "You Say" — Lauren Daigle

✦ "Known" — Tauren Wells

A PRAYER FOR TODAY

God,
Thank You for seeing me completely—and never turning away.
I've spent so long trying to be impressive, put-together, and worthy.
But You loved me before I ever got it right.
You see every frame—every moment I'd rather hide—and still call me Your own.
Help me stop performing.
Help me show up honestly.
Let my Joy grow deep in the soil of Your unconditional love.
And let me trust that I am fully known... and fully loved by you.
Amen.

Chapter 12

LIGHTNING LANE DOESN'T ALWAYS WORK

DAY ONE
WHAT MISSED PLANS
CAN TEACH US ABOUT
TRUSTING GOD'S TIMING

I had the perfect plan.

Rides, snacks, the parade, dinner—and of course, capping it all off with Happily Ever After. I even scored a Lightning Lane for Tiana's Bayou Adventure.

(And yes, I still call them FastPasses. Old habits die hard.)

It was the kind of park day that made me feel like a planning genius.

Until Lightning Lane said: "Nope."

I was scanned in, standing in the queue, almost ready to board... and the ride went down. Just like that.

Around me? Grumbles. Frustration. Certainly someone dramatically claiming their vacation was ruined. And I get it. That Lightning Lane was part of the plan.

And now the plan was officially trashed.

Sure, we could come back later if the ride reopened. But let's be honest—when your perfect plan gets even slightly rerouted, it can feel like a full-on derailment.

And I should be used to this by now.
Because honestly? Life hasn't gone according to my "perfect plan" either.

The dreams I had fresh out of college didn't go the way I imagined.
The picture I had of a wife, three kids, and a house at the beach hasn't played out.
My vision of moving to Orlando, buying a house in Golden Oak, and biking through Fort Wilderness every morning... let's just say that one's still parked in Fantasyland.

Plans fall through.
Lightning Lanes break down.
And sometimes, life reroutes you in ways that don't make sense at all.

Here's the thing: Lightning Lanes—just like life—don't always go as planned.

Sometimes, we want God to give us a FastPass through the hard stuff.
We pray like it's Genie+, expecting front-of-the-line access to the good things.
We think doing it "right" should get us there quicker.

But God isn't in the business of speed.
He's in the business of growth.
And growth often takes the long way.
We want shortcuts.
But God wants to shape something in us that shortcuts can't reach.

Let's be honest—it can be frustrating.
You make the plans. You pray the prayers. You line everything up— and then it feels like you're stuck in Standby, watching everyone else skip ahead.

You think:
"Did God forget about me?"
"Did I miss my moment?"
"Why are they getting what I've been waiting for?"

But friend—delays are not denials.
And detours aren't rejections.
They're redirections.
What feels like a detour may actually be the scenic route to
something more beautiful.

"For my thoughts are not your thoughts,
neither are your ways my ways," declares the Lord.
—Isaiah 55:8–9

"Let us not grow weary in doing good,
for at the proper time we will reap a harvest..."
—Galatians 6:9

Here's what I know:
The plans I made in my twenties didn't work out.
But oh, the life God gave me instead!

It's been richer, deeper, and more Joy-filled than I ever could've
dreamed up on my own.

God's plan may not match your timing—but you can trust that He
makes beautiful things, even from broken timelines.

Faith is trusting God when the answer is "yes"—

and still trusting Him when the answer is "not yet"... or even "no."

It's believing that you didn't miss your shot—you're simply being
led toward something better

So yes—feel the disappointment when your plans fall through.
That's real. That's honest.
But don't give up on the good just because it hasn't come yet.

God is never late.
Even when your reservation gets canceled.

Joy isn't always loud and instant. Sometimes it shows up in the quiet confidence that you're still being guided—especially when the plan falls apart.

Sometimes He takes the long way—
So you can arrive healed, ready, and whole.

And when that day comes?
You won't just be on the right ride—
You'll be exactly where you were always meant to be.

Pause + Ponder

Let these questions invite deeper reflection:

✦ When have you felt like your "spiritual Lightning Lane" didn't work?

✦ How do you respond when plans fall through—do you lean in or pull away from God?

✦ Where might God be growing you in the waiting?

✦ Have you ever looked back and seen the beauty in a detour?

A BLESSING FOR THE ONE STUCK IN THE STANDBY LINE

May you know that God hasn't forgotten your place in line.
May you trust His timing, even when the wait feels long.
May you believe that what He's preparing is better than what you planned.
And when it feels like everyone else is passing you by,
May you rest in this truth:
You are not late. You are being led.

DAY TWO
LIVING IT OUT: TRUSTING
GOD IN THE STANDBY

There's something humbling about watching everyone else breeze past you in the Lightning Lane... while you're stuck waiting.

You planned. You thought it all out.

You did everything "right."

And still—here you are. Delayed. Disappointed. Wondering if God's even paying attention.

But here's the truth:

God's timing doesn't operate on a schedule you can download to your app.

He's not falling behind.

He's forming something.

We want front-of-the-line access to our dreams.

We want shortcuts to the breakthrough.

But faith doesn't come from skipping the hard parts.

It's built in the wait.

Isaiah 55:8–9 reminds us that God's ways are higher than ours.

His plans aren't just different—they're better.

And often? They're slower.

Not to punish us, but to prepare us.

Delays aren't denials.

Detours aren't mistakes.

They're holy reminders that God is working behind the scenes—even when the Lightning Lane breaks down.

Galatians 6:9 says there is a proper time for the harvest.
And that "proper time" is never early—but it's always right.

So what if this season of waiting isn't holding you back... but holding you together?
What if this isn't wasted time—but sacred time?

Friend, don't mistake delay for absence.
God hasn't forgotten you.
He's just writing a better story than the one you planned.

Read

> *"'For my thoughts are not your thoughts,*
> *neither are your ways my ways,' declares the Lord."*
> **—Isaiah 55:8**

> *"Let us not become weary in doing good, for at the proper time*
> *we will reap a harvest if we do not give up."*
> **—Galatians 6:9**

Reflect

Use these questions to guide your journaling:

✦ What plans in your life feel like they've stalled or fallen apart?

✦ How have you seen God's faithfulness show up through past detours or delays?

✦ Where is He asking you to trust Him—even when you don't understand the wait?

Write freely. Trust grows in the honest places.

Respond

Try one or more of these intentional steps today:

✦ Name your "wait." Write it down. Speak it aloud to God. Tell Him what feels stuck—and then surrender it into His timing.

✦ Celebrate someone else's breakthrough. Rejoicing with others reminds your heart that God is still working—even if your moment hasn't come yet.

✦ Choose Joy. What does choosing Joy during a time of waiting look like for you? How can you tangibly choose Joy during a time of waiting?

Songs for Today

✦ "While I Wait" — Lincoln Brewster
✦ "God of the Breakthrough" — Crossroads Music

A PRAYER FOR TODAY

Lord,
I'm tired of waiting.
Tired of feeling behind.
But today I choose to trust You in the delay.
Even when the door closes. Even when the plan falls through.
Remind me that You see more than I do—and You're leading me somewhere better.
Help me believe that the wait is not wasted.
Let Joy rise in my heart, not because I've arrived, but because You are with me in the wait.
Help me Choose Joy.
Remind me..
I'm not forgotten.
I'm not overlooked.
I'm exactly where You want me to be.
Amen.

Chapter 13

THE RESORT RESET: FINDING JOY IN THE STILLNESS

DAY ONE
WHAT DISNEY RESORT DAYS TEACH US ABOUT REST, RENEWAL & REALIGNMENT

I used to wear my Disney stamina like a badge of honor—up before sunrise, down Main Street before the crowds, chasing magic until long after the fireworks faded.

Rope Drop was my mantra.

And by rope drop, I mean showing up an hour early to snag perfect castle photos, browse the shops before the crowds hit, and be one of the first to race through the mountains.

Then, after fireworks? I'd squeeze in a few more rides while everyone else shuffled toward the exit.
It was a day packed with magic and pixie dust—sun up to well past sundown.

If you've been there, you know.
It's exhausting.
They even have a name for it: Disney Tired.

But then... I discovered the quiet magic of a Resort Day.
And it was beautiful.

At first it felt wrong—like I was breaking some sacred Disney rule. Who sits by the pool when there are rides to ride and parades to catch?

But the more I leaned in, the more I discovered: resort days are one of my favorite parts of doing Disney.

The first time I tried it was at Disney's Saratoga Springs. I spent the day by the pool, a few hours at the spa, some time in the hot tub, and even sat in my room watching Stacey on the resort TV tell me the seven things I should be out doing.

But instead of feeling guilty... I felt alive again.
Rested. Restored. Even Joyful.

I loved it so much, I did it again the next day—breakfast on the balcony, hours of reading by the pool, a long nap, and nowhere to be.

Meanwhile, I couldn't help but think of all those people waiting in long lines—while the real magic was right here, in the sunshine and peace.

To this day, I tell everyone: build in at least one Resort Day—maybe two.

I realized something that made everything more spectacular:
Resort days aren't about skipping the magic.
They're about soaking in the magic that's already all around you.

And that same truth applies to your faith.

Rope-drop-to-fireworks living—whether at Disney or in real life—will wear you down.

Life demands so much of us.
We pride ourselves on hustle.
We glorify busy.
We feel guilty if we're not producing. (Or is that just me?)

But God calls us to something different.

He doesn't just allow rest—He commands it.
Because He knows how badly we need it.

"Remember the Sabbath day by keeping it holy."
—Exodus 20:8

"Come to me, all who are weary and burdened, and I will give you rest."
—Matthew 11:28

Rest isn't laziness.

It's worship.

Trust.

A quiet way of saying:

"You're still God—even when I stop trying to run the show."

When I finally slowed down enough to really rest at Saratoga
Springs, I discovered something beautiful:
When we pause, we see clearly again.
When we rest, we're reminded of who we are—and who God is.
When we stop striving, we realize: He was already here all along.

When we're still, our direction returns.

Think of your quiet time with God like checking into a beautiful
resort.
You arrive at a space He's already prepared just for you.
You unpack the heaviness you've been carrying.
You breathe deep.
And you're reminded: You're His. And He delights in you—even here.

Resting with Him realigns our hearts.
It opens space for Him to speak, to heal, to refill.

And maybe... that's where Joy lives.
Not in the rushing, but in the resting.
Not in the results, but by being.
Not in the noise, but in the quiet confidence that you're already
cared for.

So yes—I'm asking you to add something to your schedule this week:
Time to rest.
Time to simply be.
Time to soak in the presence of the One who holds you together.

So lay it all down—by the pool, at His feet, wherever you are.

Unpack your worries.

Float for a while in the grace that's been holding you all along.

Pause + Ponder

When was the last time I truly rested—without guilt or pressure?

Do I believe God still loves me when I'm not busy "doing"?

What would it look like to build regular "Resort Reset" moments into my spiritual life?

Where might God be asking me to slow down... so He can speak?

A Blessing: For the One Who Needs Permission to Rest

May you remember: rest is not weakness—it's wisdom.
May you slow down long enough to hear God whisper again.
May your soul exhale, your heart soften, and your spirit be refilled.
And may you rediscover the kind of Joy that doesn't come from rushing—
but from resting in the One who holds it all.

DAY TWO
LIVING IT OUT:
REST IS STILL HOLY
● ●

Rest doesn't often make our to-do lists.
It's not loud or urgent.
It doesn't flash like a notification or ding like a text.

But rest is sacred.
And more than that—it's *commanded*.

We live in a world that equates busyness with value.
If you're not hustling, you're falling behind.
If you're not producing, you're slacking.
If you pause for too long, you might miss something.

But Scripture paints a different picture:
Rest isn't what you do when everything else is done—
It's what you *begin* from.

In Exodus, God doesn't suggest a break. He *commands* Sabbath.
And Jesus—God in the flesh—often slipped away from the crowd
to rest.
If He needed rest, what makes us think we can thrive without it?

When you slow down—like on a quiet Resort Day—something
shifts.
You hear things you've been too rushed to notice.
You feel the weight you've been too busy to name.
You breathe deeper.
You remember who you are.

Rest isn't just a luxury. It's a declaration:
"I trust God enough to stop."
"I believe He's still working—even when I'm not."

Joy doesn't only live in mountaintop moments and fireworks finales.
Sometimes it shows up by the pool.
In the quiet.
In the nap.
In the stillness where God reminds you:
You are already loved. You don't have to earn it.

Read

"Come to me, all who are weary and burdened, and I will give you rest."
— Matthew 11:28

"In repentance and rest is your salvation,
in quietness and trust is your strength..."
— Isaiah 30:15

Reflect

Let these questions guide your time with God:

✦ Do I view rest as something holy—or something optional?

✦ What might I need to lay down this week so I can truly pause?

✦ What would it look like to rest *with* God, not just *from* life?

Write freely. Let honesty lead you back to stillness.

Respond

Here are a few simple ways to practice a spiritual "Resort Reset" today:

✦ Block 30 minutes for rest. Turn off your phone. Sit with God. Don't multitask. Just *be*.

✦ Take a slow walk. Let creation remind you that God never rushes—and yet He holds everything together.

✦ Pick a verse about rest and meditate on it. Read it slowly. Let it become your permission slip to breathe.

Songs for Today

✦ *"Breathe"* — Johnny Diaz

✦ *"Still"* — Amanda Cook

✦ *"Worthy Of It All"* — Shane & Shane

A Prayer for Today

Lord,
I've been moving too fast.
Trying to keep up. Trying to hold it all together.
But I hear You whispering, "Come sit with Me."
Help me stop striving long enough to hear Your voice again.
Give me courage to pause.
To rest.
To believe that You're still holding everything together—even when I let go.
Fill the quiet with Your presence.
Let Joy rise in the stillness.
And let me remember that being with You is always enough.
Amen.

Chapter 14

CHOOSE JOY — LETTING GO TO MAKE ROOM FOR WHAT MATTERS

DAY ONE
AT DISNEY, IT'S ALMOST IMPOSSIBLE TO LEAVE A RIDE WITHOUT BEING FUNNELED THROUGH A GIFT SHOP.

Pirates of the Caribbean? You're funneled straight into a sea of plastic swords, pirate hats, and stuffed Jack Sparrows.

Space Mountain? Glow-in-the-dark T-shirts and astronaut Mickeys wait to launch home with you.

Even when there isn't a shop at the exit, one is always nearby — brimming with bubble wands, plushes, candy, and shiny new tumblers begging for space in your bag.

I've walked through those shops more times than I can count — and it's always fun to watch how people light up when they find the perfect souvenir. But sometimes, I can't help but notice how much people pile on — strollers overflowing with bags, parents juggling kids and merchandise, arms so full they can barely take another step.

And isn't that just like life?

Every season leaves us carrying something — souvenirs of joy, but also baggage we were never meant to hold.
The question isn't whether we'll pick things up — but whether we'll choose wisely what's worth keeping.

At Disney, it's obvious when the suitcase won't close. You sit on it. You play Tetris trying to fit everything back in. You wonder why you brought home so much that you don't even really need.

Life, though?
We don't always realize how heavy our bags have become until we feel the weight pressing down on us.

Honest confession: I'm bad at letting go. Drawers, closets, even a whole "junk room" — full of things I can't quite part with, even though they only take up space.

And spiritually? We do the same.
We carry things that once felt important... but now only weigh us down.
Wounds. Regrets. Bitterness.
We clutch them like painful souvenirs, not realizing they crowd out the Joy God longs to give.

On the flip side, there are blessings — memories, lessons, moments of Joy — that are always worth keeping.
They make the load lighter.
They remind us who we really are.

But here's the truth: you don't have to carry everything.
You were never meant to.

Hebrews 12:1 says it beautifully:

> *"Let us throw off everything that hinders and*
> *the sin that so easily entangles..."*

And Philippians 3:13 reminds us:

"...forgetting what is behind and straining toward what is ahead."

Guilt? Already forgiven.
Shame? Redeemed.
Bitterness? Not yours to bear anymore.
That voice in your head that replays past mistakes? You don't have to let it stay rent-free.

Carrying all of that and trying to hold onto Joy at the same time? Impossible.

Like light and dark.
Like hot and cold.
Like oil and water — they can't exist in the same space.

Joy is a choice.
Every day.
Every moment.
And when you're standing in the "gift shop" of your heart trying to decide what to keep?
Choose Joy.
Always choose Joy.

Because Joy travels light.

It leaves room for what matters.

It frees your hands to hold the blessings God keeps giving.

Picture this:

At the end of a long Disney trip, you're back in your resort room, suitcase open. You sort through everything — some things make you smile as you fold them neatly. Others you set aside, realizing they're just unnecessary weight.

That's what faith invites you to do every day.
Sit with God.
Open up the suitcase of your soul.

Let Him help you sort it out.
Keep what's worth keeping — and leave the rest with Him.

You don't have to carry every souvenir from every stop.
Even Disney lets you ship things home — but God?
He lets you leave it all at His feet.

So choose Joy.

Release what weighs you down.

Pack what brings peace, hope, and life.

Travel light — and make space for what matters most.

Pause + Ponder

✦ What am I carrying right now that feels heavy or unnecessary?

✦ Are there things God is asking me to release?

✦ What blessings or lessons do I want to "pack" for the next season?

✦ If my spiritual life were a suitcase, what would I want it to contain?

A BLESSING: FOR THE ONE CHOOSING WHAT TO CARRY

May your hands open to release what was never meant to stay.

May your heart make space for Joy, peace, and hope.

May you trust God to carry what you cannot.

And as you step into the next chapter — lighter, freer, full of what truly matters —

may you boldly, beautifully, and wholeheartedly...

Choose Joy — and carry it with you wherever you go.

DAY TWO
LIVING IT OUT: PACK LIGHT, CHOOSE JOY

· · · · · · · · · · · · · · · · ·

We carry so much.

Schedules packed tight. Hearts full of pressure. Minds cluttered with "what ifs" and "should haves."

And sometimes, we're so used to the weight, we forget it's optional.

Joy doesn't need much room.
But it does need space.
Space you can't give it if your arms are full of everything else.

Just like leaving a Disney gift shop with an overflowing stroller and three new bubble wands you didn't plan for—life has a way of handing us extra "souvenirs."
Some are beautiful.
Some are burdens.

But the same truth applies:
You don't have to carry it all.

God invites you to regularly open your spiritual suitcase—lay it all out—and ask Him, "What's worth keeping?"

Hebrews 12:1 says to throw off whatever hinders.
Philippians 3:13 tells us to forget what's behind and press forward.
Why? Because heaviness and Joy can't walk in step for long.

There's freedom in letting go.
There's clarity in traveling light.

And there's deep, sustaining Joy in knowing your hands are open to receive what actually matters.

So today, release what's weighing you down.
Name it. Lay it down.
And make room for the Joy that's already waiting to take its place.

Read

*"Let us throw off everything that hinders and
the sin that so easily entangles..."*
— Hebrews 12:1

"...forgetting what is behind and straining toward what is ahead..."
— Philippians 3:13

Reflect

Use these questions to help unpack your heart:

✦ What are you holding onto that God never asked you to carry?

✦ Where do you feel weighed down emotionally or spiritually?

✦ What would "traveling light" look like in your walk with God?

Be honest. Light begins with release. Write out what you need to let go of.

Respond

Here are a few practical ways to choose Joy and let go today:

+ Write a release letter. Journal one thing you've been carrying too long. Write it down, pray over it, then tear it up or toss it. Let it go.
+ Do a gratitude swap. For every burden you name, write down a blessing you're choosing to carry instead.
+ Clean one space today. A drawer, a corner, a desktop. As you physically clear clutter, ask God to clear what's crowding your heart too.

Songs for Today

+ "Cast My Cares" — Finding Favour
+ "Joy of the Lord" — Rend Collective

A PRAYER FOR TODAY

Father,
I've been carrying too much.
Some of it You never asked me to hold.
Today, I want to travel lighter.
Help me lay down what weighs me down—and cling to what brings life.
Remind me that I don't have to do it all or hold it all together.
You are my peace.
You are my portion.
And today, I choose to make room for Joy. I choose Joy.
Amen.

Chapter 15:

BUILT TO WITHSTAND

DAY ONE
WHAT A STORM-SOAKED CITY & A STANDING CASTLE TEACH US ABOUT RESILIENT FAITH

Flying into Orlando from Nashville, I spent the entire flight lost in that final-day-dreaming stage of Disney vacation planning — imagining lazy laps around Typhoon Lagoon's river, rope-drop mornings, and fireworks painting the night sky over Wishes and Illuminations.

As the plane descended, I did what I always do: pressed my face to the window, hoping to catch a glimpse of something — anything — Disney. Maybe Cinderella Castle glittering in the sun.

But instead of magic, all I saw was blue.
A sea of blue tarps stretched out below me, covering roof after roof like bandages. Not just in one neighborhood, but everywhere — miles and miles of damage.

Hurricane Charley had torn through Central Florida just a month earlier, and though I'd seen headlines, I wasn't prepared for the sight of such widespread destruction.

And honestly? My first selfish thought was: Is Disney World even okay?

After landing, I picked up my rental car and drove straight to the resort.
But the strangest thing happened: the second I passed under the "Walt Disney World" archway, it was like entering another world.

Gone were the tarps and fallen trees. The roads were clean. The landscaping was immaculate. The castle? Standing tall, sparkling like nothing had ever happened.

It was as if the storm had never touched this place — but deep down, I knew it had. The winds had blown. The rains had come. And yet, here it stood.

Later on that trip, I learned why.

Disney designs its buildings to withstand hurricanes. They invest in deep, secure foundations, underground utilities, reinforced structures. They don't just hope storms won't come — they plan for them.

But there was another detail that stuck with me even more.
I noticed fallen trees along some of the roads and walkways. A cast member explained: because of heavy irrigation to keep the grounds lush and green, the trees never develop deep roots.

Shallow roots look sturdy on sunny days — but when the winds roar, they fall.

And I couldn't help but think: That'll preach.

Growing up, Vacation Bible School taught me the song:

The wise man built his house upon the Rock… and it did not fall.

It took me years to understand: it wasn't just about where you build your house — it's about where you build your life.

Life sends storms. Loss. Disappointment. Betrayal. Sickness.
Faith doesn't erase the storm — but it gives you something solid to stand on when it hits.

"The wise man built his house on the rock... and it did not fall."
— Matthew 7:24–27

*"See, I lay a stone... a tested stone, a precious
cornerstone for a sure foundation."*
— Isaiah 28:16

Here's what I've learned:
What's under you — your foundation — matters more than what's around you.
Your surroundings will change. Your circumstances will shift.
But if your life is built on Jesus, you can withstand even the fiercest winds.

Joy doesn't come from what's around you — it comes from what's under you.

God doesn't promise to calm every storm — but He does promise to be your shelter through it.

For me, my shaky foundations have often been my own performance, my need for control, my perfectionism. Maybe yours have been different — but you know where you've been standing.

Let go of the sandy foundations.
Plant your feet firmly on the Rock.
Build your identity, your hope, your worth, your dreams — all of it — on Him.

You'll never control the weather.

But you can choose where you plant your feet.

When Christ is your foundation, you may shake — but you won't shatter.

Your peace won't depend on clear skies.

Your Joy won't blow away with the winds.

Stand firm.

The storms will come.

But so will His strength.

And He is holding you steady..

Pause + Ponder

+ What storm in my life has revealed cracks in my foundation?

+ Have I been building on temporary or unsteady things?

+ What does it mean to truly anchor my life in Christ?

+ How might my story change if I fully trusted His strength to hold me?

A BLESSING: FOR THE ONE STILL STANDING AFTER THE STORM

May you know: the winds may howl and the rains may fall —

but you will not be moved when your hope is in Him.

May the cracks in your story become the places where His light shines through.

May your strength come not from avoiding the storm —

but from knowing the One who holds you steady within it.

And when others wonder how you're still standing,

may your life quietly, confidently, and Joyfully whisper:

Christ is my firm foundation, the Rock on which I stand.

DAY TWO
LIVING IT OUT: STORM-TESTED, SAVIOR-SECURE

When the storm hits, your foundation gets exposed.
You can't fake depth when the winds start to howl.

That's something the blue tarps over Central Florida taught me that day—some roofs weren't ready. Some roots weren't deep. But Cinderella Castle? Still standing.

That kind of resilience doesn't happen by accident.

It's built over time—layer by layer, decision by decision, prayer by prayer.

And the same is true with faith.

Jesus said the wise person "hears these words of mine and puts them into practice."
Not just knows them. Not just quotes them. But lives them.

Because it's not the sunshine that proves your foundation.
It's the storm.

Here's the good news:
Your ability to withstand the winds has nothing to do with your strength—
and everything to do with where you're standing.

If your life is anchored in Christ—
you might bend, you might wobble, you might even fall to your knees—
but you will not be destroyed.

Not because you're strong,
but because He is.

Read

*"The rain came down, the streams rose, and the winds blew
and beat against that house; yet it did not fall, because it
had its foundation on the rock."*
— Matthew 7:25

"We have this hope as an anchor for the soul, firm and secure."
— Hebrews 6:19

Reflect

Use these questions to examine your spiritual foundation:

✦ What storm in your life revealed a shaky foundation?

✦ What have you learned about God's strength when your own ran out?

✦ What spiritual habits (prayer, Scripture, community, rest) help you dig deeper roots?

✦ How would your response to hard times change if your peace didn't depend on the weather?

Respond

Try one of these practical ways to reinforce your foundation today:

✦ Journal your anchor verse. Choose one Scripture you can cling to when storms come. Write it down and place it somewhere you'll see often.

✦ Reflect on a past storm. What did you survive that once felt impossible? What did it teach you about God's steadiness?

✦ Pray the cracks. Whatever's been exposed lately—fear, doubt, exhaustion—bring it to God. Ask Him to meet you there and strengthen what's weak.

Songs for Today

✦ "Firm Foundation (He Won't)" — Cody Carnes
✦ "You Will Remain" — All Sons & Daughters

A PRAYER FOR TODAY

Jesus,
When the winds howl and the skies grow dark, remind me where to stand.
Not on performance, or perfection, or pretending—but on You.
You are my firm foundation. My Rock. My shelter in the storm.

When life feels unsteady, anchor my heart in truth.
When I'm tempted to fear, plant my feet in faith.
And when the pressure mounts to give up or give in,
remind me: I can still Choose Joy.

Not because the storm is over,
but because You're with me in the middle of it.

Help me build a life that lasts—deeply rooted, storm-tested, and Savior-secure.
Let my Joy rise not from easy days,
but from the unshakable hope I have in You.

Amen.

EPILOGUE:
THE JOY AHEAD

As you close this book, I hope you've caught a glimpse of the kind of Joy that can carry you through anything — the kind that shines on Main Street, echoes in quiet resort moments, and stands firm when the storms come.

This journey wasn't about pretending life is perfect. It wasn't about escaping into Fantasyland.
It was about noticing what's already true — that Joy is possible here, now, and always because of the One who never changes.

The truth is: you're going to leave here and walk back into a world that still has hard days. You'll still face lines that feel too long, storms that feel too strong, and moments that feel anything but magical.

But you'll also walk back into a world where God is still good.
Where His mercies are still new every morning.
Where His presence still goes with you, even when the path winds or the skies darken.

So as you step into the days ahead, don't forget:
You get to choose Joy — every day.

And you never choose it alone.

Take what you've learned here. Sit with it. Live it. Share it.
Let the Joy of the Lord be your strength, your song, your anchor, and your light.

And when the winds pick up, when the world feels heavy, when others wonder how you're still standing —
may your life quietly, boldly, beautifully whisper:

Christ is my firm foundation. The Rock on which I stand. The Joy no storm can take away.

Here's to the Joy ahead — and God who holds you through it all.

ABOUT THE AUTHOR

Bonnie Cribbs is a former Walt Disney World Cast Member who believes Joy is always worth chasing—and choosing. With a deep love for faith, storytelling, and all things Disney, Bonnie blends biblical truth with park experiences to encourage others to live wide-eyed, full-hearted lives rooted in Christ.

As the founder of Mouse Marketplace and host of the weekly Park & Heart email series, Bonnie brings magic and encouragement to thousands of readers and Disney fans every week. He also leads the Mouse Marketplace Facebook Group, a thriving online community of over 76,000 members known for their kindness, generosity, and commitment to lifting others up.

When he's not creating joyful apparel, delivering resort gift baskets, or planning his next walk in the parks, Bonnie can be found watching Hallmark movies, cheering for kindness, or dreaming up new ways to bring Light to the world.

You can connect with Bonnie at www.mousemarketplace.com and follow along on Instagram @MouseMarketplace or TikTok @ mousemarketplace.com

www.ingramcontent.com/pod-product-compliance
Lightning Source LLC
Chambersburg PA
CBHW070445090426
42735CB00012B/2468